Trilogy Christian Publishers

A Wholly Owned Subsidary of Trinity Broadcasting Network

2442 Michelle Drive

Tustin, CA 92780

Copyright © 2020 by Marilyn Lebowitz

For information, address Trilogy Christian Publishing

Rights Department, 2442 Michelle Drive, Tustin, Ca 92780.

Trilogy Christian Publishing/ TBN and colophon are trademarks of Trinity Broadcasting Network.

For information about special discounts for bulk purchases, please contact Trilogy Christian Publishing.

Manufactured in the United States of America

10 9 8 7 6 5 4 3 2 1

Library of Congress Cataloging-in-Publication Data is available.

ISBN 978-1-64088-676-6 (Print)

ISBN 978-1-64088-677-3 (eBook)

Marilyn Lebowitz

Jesus, the Rabbi from Nazareth

Trilogy Christian Publishers

CONTENTS

It was a very hot day, but there was a breeze in the air. People were seated in large groups on a hillside, listening to a man who was dressed as a Rabbi. Even though many people surrounded Him, His voice was heard as if carried on the wind. He was talking about a kingdom—the kingdom of God.

He had their complete attention. Their eyes were focused on His face as they listened to every word He spoke. He was very different from anyone they had ever met before. As He talked to them, His eyes often looked up into the sky, as if He could see right through the clouds. He told them about His Father whom He said was in heaven.

The people were fascinated.

Josephus, a well-respected first century Jewish historian, called Jesus a wonder worker. God called Him His Son.

ACKNOWLEDGMENTS

Dedicated to the loving memory of my parents, Ruth and Irving Lebowitz. They were heartbroken when I decided to follow Jesus, but today, they are in heaven because of His mercy and grace. Each of them, shortly before they died, accepted Him, by faith, as their Mashiach or Messiah.

Jesus told the woman He met at the well in Samaria that He was the promised Messiah of Israel. Either He was lying, crazy, or telling the truth. All of Christianity crumbles if Jesus is not the Messiah of Israel. Its foundation rests on that core belief.

My heartfelt prayer is that this little book will, in some way, help to heal the many profound misunderstandings which exist.

Shalom, Marilyn Lebowitz.

"I will place salvation in Zion, for Israel my glory" (Isaiah 46:13, ESV).

My two earliest memories of my Jewish heritage were my grandmother lighting the Shabbat candles on Friday nights, and my grandfather occasionally taking me to temple. In the temple, some men were called up front to read from the Torah. They approached the Holy Book reverently with a yarmulke on their heads and a prayer shawl wrapped around their shoulders. On one of those days, something very special happened.

One of the men read from the Torah as the others had done before him. However, when he was finished reading, this man did something very different from the others. He bowed his body over the Holy Book, bent down low, and kissed the page in front of him. For some reason, even though I was very young (about eight years old), I was deeply affected by this. To this day, I don't know why. But if you were to ask me when my spiritual journey began, I would say that it began that day. It was as if God touched my shoulder and said, "I am here. Come, follow Me."

Many years later, I remember one very cloudy day in particular when I was a teenager. Sitting on some large boulders on an esplanade near the ocean's shore where I lived in Brooklyn, I looked up at the sky and said to God, "I want to know You." From that day to this one, I have been on an extraordinary journey. I traveled many different paths searching for God, and to my astonishment, He revealed Himself to me as Jesus, the long-promised Messiah of Israel, as the Jewish prophets had foretold in the Older Testament. It has been a very difficult journey, and I have had to face great challenges. However, I do believe, with all my heart, that God heard my prayer on that cloudy day so long ago and guided my wandering steps.

So how does a Jew deal with the stunning revelation that Jesus is the Messiah of Israel? Well, I knew I had to go back to the beginning where everything began, and that meant the book of beginnings—Genesis, the first book of the Torah. I realized that not having a Bible in my house or in my hand had severely limited my search for God. It was as if I had travelled all those years without a compass or a map.

The first thing I wanted to understand was how Jesus could be the Messiah of Israel when I, and most Jews, thought of Him as the God the Christians worshipped. We, of course, worshipped the God of Abraham, Isaac, and Jacob. I found the answer.

Each of us has a story to tell. I chose to share some of my experiences in a format which combines both truth and fantasy in order to, hopefully, hold your attention. The way Becky's parents were saved is exactly the way the Lord saved my parents.

We presently live in very dangerous and uncertain times. It is a very different age than when I was growing up. All of us need an anchor, hope, and the guidance of the one true North Star. I found all three in the pages of the Holy Scriptures (the Bible) sent to us from the heart of a loving and living God.

CHAPTER 1

The school bell rang, ending the classroom session for the day. Becky gathered her books and headed for the door leading to the street. Walking home—absorbed in her thoughts about an upcoming chemistry exam—she didn't see a small group of teenage girls clustered in front of a church. As she passed by, her shoulder accidently touched one of the girls. Apologizing immediately, she tried to move on. However, the girl grabbed her arm saying, "Why don't you look where you are going?" The girl noticed the Jewish star around Becky's neck and said to the others, "Hey, look who's here, one of the Christ killers."

Startled, Becky replied, "What do you mean?"

The girl snarled. "Oh, come on, don't play innocent. You know that you and your people were responsible for the death of Jesus."

"I don't know what you are talking about. Please let go of my arm," Becky replied. Afraid of an escalating confrontation, she yanked her arm free and began to run. Behind her, she could hear voices calling after her, "Christ killer, Christ killer, Christ killer."

Deeply disturbed by this event, Becky reached her home and entered the front door. Through her tears, she could see her mother preparing dinner in the kitchen. Becky quickly ran to her, explained what happened, and sat down. Putting her arm around her, her mother said, "Becky, I'm so sorry, but sometimes, these things happen to us. We are Jews. Try not to dwell on it. Those teenagers are not your friends, anyway." Becky's mother walked to the refrigerator and took out some chocolate cake and said, "Here, have some of Grandma's delicious cake. It will make you feel better."

Becky wiped her tears and ate the cake. When she finished, she gave her mother a hug and went upstairs to her bedroom. She was still upset by the unexpected experience that afternoon. She had never encountered anything like that before.

Becky sat down at her desk, opened a book, and listened to the chirping of the birds outside her bedroom window. Suddenly, there appeared a ring of radiant colors in her room. In the middle of the circle, she saw the figure of a man. His robe was white like fresh-fallen snow.

The man moved closer to her and began to speak, "Becky, I am Jesus. You don't know Me, but I have known you, even when you were in your mother's womb.[1] I saw what happened this afternoon. There is so much confusion in the world about who I am, what happened on the cross, and why I died. Most people don't understand who I am and why I came from heaven to Earth. Even most of the Jewish people don't understand. I came first to them with the gift of eternal life, but they rejected Me. It breaks My heart to know the gift they turned down and are still

1. Psalm 139:13–14.

refusing. Will you help Me reach them?"[2]

Taken aback, Becky asked, "Me? Why me?"

He answered, "Why not you? You have a tender heart, an open mind, and are not prejudiced against Me. Also, you are teachable."

Becky thought for a moment and said, "How can I possibly help you? You say you saw what happened this afternoon. Those girls are supposed to be Christians!"

Jesus said, "That's just one example of the many misunderstandings which exist between Christians and Jews. Becky, I am Jewish, too, and at one time, I was a rabbi."[3]

"How do I know that I am not dreaming?" Becky said. "You died two thousand years ago!"

"You are not dreaming, Becky. I am very much alive." Jesus, then, began to explain to her who He is, where He came from, His purpose in coming to Earth, and the meaning of the cross and the resurrection.

Becky, wide-eyed, listened to every word. When He

---

2. Psalm 139:13; John 1:11.
3. John 15:16.

finished, she asked Him, "If You want me to share this with people, how will I remember everything? This is a lot of information."

Jesus replied, "I will help you remember. As I told you, I created all there is from nothing so giving you a high-powered mind and memory is not hard for Me." He told Becky He would return again and then withdrew from the foot of her bed and reentered the swirl of many colors. He was gone.[4]

The room was still. The chirping of the birds stopped, and Becky was alone with her thoughts. She was thinking about what just happened. After a while, she could hear her mother calling her, "Becky, dinner is almost ready." She hurried downstairs.

Seated at the table were her mother, father, and her brother, Charlie. He was twenty years old—two years older than she was. Becky's mother asked her how she was feeling. Becky answered by saying, "Guess who I just saw?"

Charlie asked, "Who did you see?"

"I saw Jesus," Becky replied.

---

4. John 17:7, 14:26, 14:3.

Startled, Becky's father said, "Did you take a nap? That was just a bad dream. Becky, we don't mention that name in this house, ever!"

"Why not?" asked Becky.

Her mother answered, "We just don't, that's why."

They all ate the rest of the meal in silence.

Becky returned to her room and sat down at her desk to study for her chemistry exam. She thought, *I wonder why they don't want to talk about Him. He really was very nice, and He told me a wonderful story.*

CHAPTER 2

Becky arrived at school the next day, still thinking about her encounter with Jesus. She saw her friend, Barbara, in the hall, and they walked to their first class together.

After the morning classes, Becky went to the lunchroom where several of her friends were seated at a table. She bought some lunch and then told them about her visit from Jesus that morning.

George responded immediately, "Oh, come on, are you on drugs or something?"

Howard said, "I think you are hallucinating. Too much studying. It's fried your brain."

Most of the others at the table were silent except for Barbara who said, "How do you know she didn't see Jesus. Were you there?"

Becky looked directly at George and Howard and said, "How can you deny my experience? I am not on drugs, and I am not hallucinating. This actually happened." She then shared with them what Jesus had told her. She said that He told her that He and His Father had created the whole universe—the sun, the moon, the stars, and all the planets, including the Earth. He explained that God is comprised of the Father, Son, and the Holy Spirit. He added that He would explain that to her in more detail later.[5]

"Jesus told me that everything on the Earth at that time was very beautiful. 'There were emerald-green carpets of luscious vegetation, majestic trees, and gorgeous flowers decorating the landscape. All of this was set in the midst of vast expanses of sparkling, clear turquoise water. The rays from the sun seemed to dance on top of the water. There were birds flying in the air, lots of multicolored fish swimming in the sea, and many different kinds of

5. Genesis 1–2.

animals walking freely on the Earth, all living together in perfect harmony. I looked down on the whole creation and declared, "It is very good."[6]

"'However, I wasn't finished. My crowning achievement was when I created a man called Adam and a woman named Eve. A magnificent garden was created for them. It was a paradise called Eden. In the garden, everything they would ever need was provided. Because I loved Adam and Eve very much, I would walk and talk with them often during the day. It gave Me such joy to be close to them. That was always My heart's desire to have fellowship with the two who were made in My own image. There wasn't any sickness, death, or the presence of evil. Nothing marred My beautiful creation. However, they were given one restriction. I told them they could eat from every tree in the garden except one. They were warned that if they ate from that one forbidden tree, they would die, and the happy life they enjoyed would end. They didn't know I have a fierce enemy. His name is Satan, and he hates Me. His hatred is rooted in jealousy, and he is, by

6. Genesis 1:31.

nature, a liar, a spoiler, and a destroyer. His agenda is to destroy everything I love and create. One day, Satan entered the garden and everything changed. He tempted Eve to disobey my restriction, and then, Adam listened to Eve.' When I asked Jesus why a restriction was placed on that one tree, He told me, 'I was testing Adam and Eve's loyalty, obedience, and gratitude to Me for all I had provided for them. They were never intended to be robots. I wanted them to freely love Me as much as I loved them.'[7]

"'Satan knew all this when he entered the garden and planned his malignant strategy. His weapon of choice was deception. He chose Eve as his first target. His plan was to make her doubt what I had said and my love for her. He whispered in her ear, "Eve, did God really say that you can't eat from every tree in the Garden? You surely will not die." This was a direct contradiction of what I had told Adam and Eve and it was a lie. Satan is the Father of lies.'"[8]

Becky's friends at the lunch table were now listening to her intently. She told them that Jesus said, "This was

---

7. Genesis 1:29, 3:1.
8. Genesis 3:1–5.

the exact moment when the fall of man occurred, when Eve believed the lie of Satan rather than heeding My warning. She then offered the forbidden fruit to Adam, and he ate too."[9]

Becky continued, "Jesus told me that God says what He means and means what He says. Because of this, Adam and Eve had to be confronted with what they had done. Their disobedience was a very big disappointment to Jesus and His Father. It was a sin in their holy eyes, and sin had to be judged and punished. He said that, first, their sin had to be covered. God chose the skins of animals which were sacrificed. This was when the sacrificial system began. Jesus said, 'The wages of sin is death, and the payment is the shedding of blood.' He told me that this method was God's sovereign choice. 'It saddened Our hearts,' Jesus said, 'to have to punish them, but Our holiness and righteousness demanded it. With a very heavy heart, we set in motion a series of consequences for Adam and Eve and their descendants. It included pain in childbirth for her and toil and diminished return for him. The greatest consequence

9. Genesis 3:6.

of their sin was they would be banished from the garden and My presence and live east of Eden for the remainder of their lives.'" Becky said she could see tears forming in Jesus's eyes when He said, "Becky, that's where mankind has been living ever since—east of Eden."[10]

Becky finished talking and was looking at her friends, seeking some sort of a response. Eddie was the first to speak. He said, "Becky, how can you expect us to believe that Jesus, who lived and died two thousand years ago, came to visit you and then told you all that you just told us? And by the way," he said in a mocking tone, "haven't you heard? God is dead."

At this remark, the others at the table laughed, except for Barbara. Charlotte, however, was angry. She raised her voice and shouted at Becky, "Are you for real? Don't you know that Jews don't believe in Jesus? How dare you make up a story like this? I thought I knew you, but obviously, I don't."

Suddenly, in the midst of the tension at the lunchroom table, the classroom bell rang. Becky and her friends hurried to their next class.

10. Genesis 3:14, 16, 17, 3:21; Romans 6:23.

CHAPTER 3

After school, Barbara was waiting for Becky outside. She said to Becky, "Let's take a walk." As they walked together Barbara said, "They were a little rough on you, weren't they?"

Becky nodded saying, "Yes, they were."

Barbara replied, "You know, I read about the story of creation. It's in my father's Bible, in the very first chapter of the Torah. Do you have a Bible, Becky?"

Becky shook her head saying, "No, we don't have a Bible in my house. We are not very religious. We go to synagogue only on the High Holy days."

Barbara said, "You know, you and I never really talked about God, but I believe in Him, and I try to keep an open mind. There is so much more to life than what we see. I didn't tell you, but I am taking a yoga class right now, and it has opened my mind to consider all sorts of possibilities. The supernatural is not that unusual. Many people have experienced things that can't be explained. Don't be upset. The name of Jesus sometimes has a peculiar effect on people. You know, the funny thing is in my yoga class, sometimes, my instructor talks about Hinduism and the many gods of India. I even shared that information one time with my parents. There really wasn't much of a reaction from them. Then, one time, one of our relatives mentioned the name of Jesus for some reason, and they got all bent out of shape. It was really weird. Becky, just keep an open mind. I have to do an errand now, so I'll see you later."

As Becky walked home, she tried to sort out her feelings. She was very surprised by the reaction of her friends at school. They never behaved like this before. She kept thinking about the visit from Jesus that morning and what He told her. *How am I going to handle this?* she thought. *Maybe, I am hallucinating like Howard said. I'm Jewish. Why would Jesus, the God of the Christians, come to me?* Then, she remembered that Jesus had told her that He was Jewish too and a Rabbi. *Imagine that,* Becky thought. "A Rabbi! I didn't know that. I never thought of Jesus being Jewish. Actually," Becky said to herself, "I never really thought about Him at all. I think I am going to buy a Bible, one that contains both the Older and Newer Testaments. I want to learn more about this man called Jesus."

Becky didn't really want to go straight home. Instead, she walked to the ocean just a few blocks from her home. There was an esplanade there with huge rocks jutting out into the sea, and Becky often went there to meditate. The waves gently lapping against the rocks in a consistent rhythm was always very soothing. The sound had a timeless feeling about it—a hint of something eternal, almost as if the motion of the waves began in some faraway place, at some other time, and only reached the shoreline now.

Becky always loved the ocean. She believed, somehow,

it was directly connected to God—something He had created. Its vastness spoke of His majesty and sovereignty. She often thought about God but, more or less, in terms of Earth's natural wonders—the impressive mountains reaching toward the sky, the mystery of the ocean's powerful force, the deep, dark forests which seemed to speak of hidden magical secrets, and the stars above set like glistening jewels lighting the darkness of the night.

As Becky sat on one of the jetty's big boulders, she mulled over her experiences and the reactions of some of her friends. *So, who was this man called Jesus, a Jewish Rabbi whom some people call God? Could it be? And what could that possibly have to do with me?* she thought.

All these thoughts were tumbling around in Becky's mind when it began drizzling slightly. She lifted herself off the huge boulder and walked home.

Becky returned to find that her grandmother was visiting and helping her mother prepare dinner. Becky gave her a big hug. She loved her grandmother very much. At the dinner table, there was the usual exchange of family news.

The conversation was suddenly interrupted by her brother Charlie. "Grandma, guess who Becky saw yesterday?" Everyone at the table turned to look at Becky. She flushed and tried to avoid their stares. So Charlie spoke up again, saying, "Becky saw Jesus, and He spoke to her."

Her grandmother was startled and looked at Charlie and said, "What do you mean?"

Becky, then, tried to explain what happened. Her grandmother became very angry and said to Becky, "What is this foolishness? You don't know what you are talking about."

Becky, gathering all of her courage, defended her experience saying, "It was real, Grandma, I wasn't dreaming."

Her grandmother grew very agitated, put her fork down, and yelled at Becky, "You don't know who Jesus is. He is 'di andere eyner' [it's Yiddish, 'the other one,' which means 'He is not one of us'], and we never speak of Him, never! Because of Him, many Jewish people died, and some of them were our relatives!" Her grandmother was disturbed by the conversation, and she got up from the table and went into the living room.

Becky followed her grandmother into the other room and tried to talk to her, but her grandmother turned on the TV very loud. Becky realized that there wasn't any point in trying to explain anything further. She left the room and went upstairs to complete her homework assignment. When she was done, she turned off the light and went to sleep. She wiped away some tears from her eyes before she drifted off.

Early the next morning, as the sun was streaming into her room, she saw the colorful swirl again, and in the middle of it was Jesus. He spoke gently to her, "Becky, I understand how you feel. I felt that way, too, when I tried to talk to people. Many of them just didn't understand what I was saying. The nails which pierced My hands and feet didn't hurt as much as the rejection by many of Our people. My Father had sent Me to them first with the message of hope, love, and redemption. You see, Becky, My Father and I always had a plan for the Jewish people. But to understand this, I have to take you back a bit in history. I'm glad it's Saturday, and we have more time to talk.[11]

"After the fall in the Garden of Eden, My Father and I were heartbroken. We considered Adam and Eve as Our children. Because of what had happened in the garden, they were now separated from Us, and We missed them very much. Sin had separated Us. We knew they weren't able to come back to Us because We had set a barrier at the gate of the garden. There were cherubim [angels] with a flaming sword flashing back-and-forth, stationed there to guard the way. That was part of the consequence of Adam and Eve's disobedience. Many years passed, and Adam and Eve's children and descendants multiplied. Some of their stories are told in the Bible. But all during this time, Our hearts ached to be reunited with Our creation. So we set in motion a plan We had created since before the foundation of the world which would bring mankind back to Us. We knew mankind would be tempted in the garden and fall even before they were created.[12]

---

11. John 1:11.
12. Isaiah 59:2; Jeremiah 31:3.

"Because We are holy, and Our creation had become sinful, Our plan had to meet the demands of Our righteous justice and loving mercy. I was central to that plan. My sacrificial death on the cross is the bridge back to reconciliation between God and man and, eventually, restoration of what was lost in the garden.[13] It is the only plan which restores what was lost because My Father and I devised it. Man can't create anything which would bring him back to Us. That's a gap which can only be bridged by God alone.[14]

"At the time We decided to implement Our plan, the world had become very idolatrous and pagan. People were worshipping false gods of their own making. For example, some of them would take some wood from the forest, use part of it to heat and cook their meals, and the rest they would carve into images to be worshipped.[15]

"These images had eyes that couldn't see and ears that couldn't hear, but still, they worshipped them anyway. These images were as spiritually dead as the people who

13. Romans 5:1, 6.
14. Acts 4:12.
15. Isaiah 44:9–20.

worshipped them. And there were other horrible pagan practices of worship as well. This upset Us very much, so We chose a specific time to intervene. Out of the vast sea of humanity, We chose a small group of people—the Jewish people. Our people, Becky. They were Our sovereign choice, and Our plan was that through them, My Father, the Holy Spirit, and I would be revealed as the only true and living God [a triune God]. Entering into a very special relationship with them, We gave them the Holy Scriptures, the Law, and the prophets as a sacred trust. Our purpose in calling the Jewish people was to set them apart as Our holy people. They were to be the guardian of Our revelation and the keeper of Our Law.[16] I will explain the triune nature of God at a later time, Becky.

"I wanted them to know Me and have a relationship with Me. Then, I could send them out into the pagan world to tell the world about Me—the God of Israel, the only true and living God. And it was through the Jewish people that the Savior of the world, the Messiah of Israel, would come bringing salvation and reconciliation with

_____

16. Romans 9:4-6, 15–16.

God. I am the Messiah and God's only Son. That was the plan that was devised to bridge the gap which sin had created and bring mankind back into a relationship with God. This plan came from the depths of My heart because I missed having fellowship with My creation for such a long time. I am the One who would be the instrument whereby mankind would be reconciled to God.

Through My sacrificial death on a cross, man's sins would be forgiven, and the relationship with God that was lost in the garden would be restored. The curse of death which was placed on mankind in the garden was reversed on the cross. In other words, My death on the cross really meant that mankind was being given a second chance."[17]

Becky interrupted. "So what happened? What went wrong? Why don't most of the Jewish people believe that You are the Messiah? And why is my grandmother so angry at You?"

"There are many reasons, Becky," Jesus replied, "but the main reason is that Satan interfered with My plan. He can't overrule My plans, but I allow him to test people's

17. Jonah 1:1-3; Rom 5:1.

hearts. So he blinded them to the truth about My Father and Me. He confused them by filling their minds and hearts with lies. And like Adam and Eve, they believed the lies rather than Me.[18]

"Satan deceived the Jewish people into believing that I, Jesus, was their enemy. Instead of being someone to be drawn to and a symbol of life, Satan made sure that, in their minds, I became someone to flee from and a symbol of death. Most of them still believe that lie.[19]

"Becky, as you begin your spiritual journey with Me, always remember that Satan presents lies as truth. He is the master counterfeiter and the father of lies!"

Jesus continued. "When I taught the people on the temple steps, the religious leaders were inside the temple reading the Scriptures and praying. The Scriptures spoke of Me, their promised Messiah, but when they saw Me teaching or performing miracles, they didn't make the connection. That's because Satan blinded their eyes. And because they couldn't see clearly, neither could most

---

18. John 8:44–45.
19. John 8:48–49, 59.

of the Jewish people. They were depending on their spiritual leaders for guidance and direction. Tragically, they failed them.[20]

"One day, I was sitting on a hill overlooking Jerusalem, and I was so sad, I began to weep. Even though in My humanity, it hurt to be rejected. I was weeping mainly for Our people. I knew what they were turning down, what they would be losing for all eternity.[21]

"I was bringing them an immense gift, offering them the opportunity to have their sins forgiven and the gates of heaven open for them. But they didn't understand. They just didn't see it. My only comfort that day was that I knew the end of the story. My Father and I will remain faithful to the promises We made to them when Our relationship began, and many, many Jewish people will come to faith in Me. They will finally accept Me as their Messiah and fulfill their original calling and purpose which is to let the whole world know that there is only one true and living God."

Becky said, "That sounds so wonderful. I borrowed

20. John 5:39–40; Matthew 15:14, 23:16, 23:24.
21. Matthew 23:37–39.

a Bible from the library yesterday and started to skim through the pages quickly. I wanted to be able to talk to You about what happened. I never read or heard the whole story. I read the first book of the Newer Testament written by Matthew. I was surprised to learn that he was Jewish, too, and he was writing to the many Jewish people who were Your followers."

Jesus interrupted by saying, "Yes, Matthew was Jewish. And except for Luke, who was a Greek physician, all of the writers of the whole Bible—both the Older and Newer Testaments—were Jewish."[22]

"Really?" said Becky. "How many people know this?"

"Well, it's not a secret," replied Jesus. "There is a lot of work to be done, Becky. Satan's strategy today hasn't really changed. He wants to keep the world in darkness, away from the truth and the light. He doesn't want people to know a lot of things. First, he doesn't want them to know that he exists. He wants them to believe that because he is invisible, he is fictional. Second, he wants to blind them to who I really am so that they won't come to Me and be set

22. Matthew 23:37–39; Romans 11:7–8, 17, 25–27.

free from the cycle of life and death."

Becky, puzzled, asked, "What is the cycle of life and death?"[23]

Jesus answered, "The cycle of life and death began after the fall in the garden. It was the consequence of Adam and Eve's sin. Man is born, he lives, and then, he dies. No one escapes it. Everyone dies. Since I carried everyone's sins to the cross and paid the penalty for mankind's sins, My death on the cross broke the cycle. I overcame death. Everyone who believes in Me will no longer have to die. They will live eternally with Me in heaven."[24]

Becky asked, "What do you mean, they don't have to die. You just said everyone dies."

Jesus answered, "They will die physically, but spiritually, they will be raised, as I was, to live forever."

Becky responded, "So You actually died, and now, You are here with me now. How is that possible?"

Jesus answered, "Yes, Becky, I actually died physically. I was dead, and they placed My body in a tomb, and then,

---

23. 2 Corinthians 11:14.
24. Genesis 2:17; John 11:25–26; Revelation 2:11, 20:6.

My Father raised Me from the dead, leaving an empty tomb.[25] When He did that, He was telling the whole world that mankind's sin debt was paid in full, and the barrier between sinful man and a Holy God was removed. Actually, Becky, mankind's greatest legacy is an empty tomb![26]

"There is another thing Satan doesn't want people to know and that is that I am the only One who has the keys to the kingdom of heaven. They were given to Me by My Father, and no one enters Heaven but through Me and the way of the cross. Only the forgiven will enter the kingdom of God, and forgiveness can only be found through accepting My death on the cross as the payment for sin."[27]

Becky asked, "Why can forgiveness be found only that way?"

Jesus replied, "Because it was on the cross and only there that the final and complete atonement for man's sins was made. What happened there was an exchange between My Father and Myself."[28]

---

25. 1 Corinthians 15:1–4.
26. John 20:1–3.
27. Revelation 1:18; John 14:6.
28. Romans 3:25.

Becky asked, "What actually happened there?"

Jesus said, "In the garden, Adam and Eve enjoyed a wonderful relationship with Me, but after the fall, everything changed. All of Adam's descendants are born with a sin nature and are spiritually separated from Me. Adam was the representative head of the human race, and when he fell, it affected all of humanity. Because of their disobedience, men and women are born spiritually blind. Part of the blindness is that they don't know they are blind. Unless they come to a place of faith in Me and receive a 'second birth' [which is a spiritual birth], they will never be able to have a relationship with Me. Every person needs a new heart and My spirit living in him to enjoy that relationship.[29]

"Although the punishment for Adam and Eve's disobedience was just and righteous, My Father and I were not happy being separated from those made in Our image. So in Our infinite love and wisdom, We established a sacrificial system which involved a blood sacrifice, whereby a sinful person could approach us and be reconciled to us.

29. John 3:3.

This is clearly seen in the Torah. This was written with Me in mind all the time. In the third book of the Torah—Leviticus—you will read, 'For the life of a creature is in the blood, and I have given it to you to make atonement for yourselves on the altar; for it is the blood that makes atonement for one's life' [Leviticus 17:11, NIV]. In the tabernacle in the wilderness and later in the temple, the blood sacrifices all pointed to My sacrifice on the cross."[30]

Becky interrupted. "But why blood?"

Jesus answered, "Because of the penalty of sin. In the garden, We had told Adam and Eve that if they disobeyed Our instructions, they would die. They did disobey, and We, true to Our word, imposed the penalty of death, just as We had warned them. Elsewhere in the Scriptures, it is written, 'The wages of sin is death' [Romans 6:23, NIV]."

Becky asked, "Isn't that kind of harsh?"

"I am a holy and righteous God, Becky, and sin is a powerful, corrupting force. However, I am also kind and loving. That is why I paid the penalty for sin and paid it

---

30. John 1:29.

in full.[31] The way back to Me is only through the sacrificial system of atonement. In order for the penalty for sin to be paid, blood had to be shed. 'The shedding of blood' means someone has to die. In the beginning, animals were sacrificed. Later, I was laid on the altar which was the cross. The animal sacrifices were just a foreshadowing of a future event.[32]

"In the sacrificial system, which is described in the Torah, we see that one's sins are transferred to an animal which is slain. In Leviticus 1:4, it is written that when someone brings an animal as an offering for sin, 'He is to lay his hand on the head of the burnt offering, and it will be accepted on his behalf to make atonement for him.' Once a year, on the Day of Atonement, the high priest selects a goat to carry away the sins of the people. It is called a 'scapegoat.' When I died on the cross, I was the scapegoat for the sins of the whole world. But no one took My life from Me, Becky. I laid it down willingly. It wasn't the nails which held Me to the cross. It was My love for all mankind

---

31. Romans 6:23; John 6:37.
32. Hebrews 7:27, 9:12, 26; 10:2, 10.

which kept Me there."[33]

Becky replied, "That's amazing. I'm beginning to understand that the sacrificial plan began in the Torah and was carried forward all the way into the Newer Testament. There is a connection between the 'scapegoat' in the Older Testament and Your death on the cross in the Newer Testament. You know, I spent a lot of time in Hebrew school, but now, I feel that I was told only half the story."

"It wasn't intentional, Becky. Your instructors worked with what they had received from their teachers. My prophet, Jeremiah, wrote in the Older Testament that a future time would come when I would enter into a New Covenant with the Jewish people. It is written, 'The time is coming, declares the Lord, when I will make a New Covenant with the house of Israel and with the house of Judah' [Jeremiah 31:31, ESV].

"You are very insightful, Becky. In Hebrew school, you did get only half the story. It was cut off in the middle. The story I was telling did not end in the Older Testament. My story continues and concludes in the Newer Testament,

33. Leviticus 16:8–10; John 10:17–18.

in the book of Revelation. The whole Bible, which contains the Older and Newer Testament, is one book and has one author. I am the author. I am the author. I am the storyteller. I used men as My instruments to write and tell people about Me, My ways, and My redemptive plan. It was written progressively, in unfolding stages, because I chose to tell the story by slowly foreshadowing future events and people. For example, when you go into a dark room to develop a negative of a photograph, it isn't clear right away. At first, the picture is cloudy and only partially seen. Then, in time, it becomes clearer and clearer until, finally, you can see the complete image. When the picture is fully developed, the whole image, with all of its details, can be clearly seen."[34]

Jesus continued, "Do you remember the story of Cain and Abel? Here, we see a glimpse of My redemptive plan. Abel brought Me an offering of the firstlings of the flock to be sacrificed. Cain brought Me an offering of the fruit of the Earth. By bringing a lamb to Me as a sacrifice, Abel was saying, 'God, if you say I am a sinner, then I am a sinner. If you say the only way I can approach you,

34. 2 Peter 1:20–21.

a holy God, is by a blood sacrifice, then, that is what I will do. You are God.' Abel was humble, obedient, and recognized My sovereignty.

"Cain, on the other hand, rejected My instruction and said, in essence, 'I know better. I love God too, and I will bring Him the fruit of my labor which represents my 'works,' and it is the best that the Earth can produce.'

"What Cain was really saying was, 'God, you say I am a sinner. But I am not really a sinner, I am a good person. You say, a blood sacrifice is necessary to approach you, but that is repugnant. Wouldn't a big, beautiful basket of fruit and vegetables be more pleasing in your sight?' So Cain did what was right in his own eyes. But he forgot that the gift he was bringing, the fruit of the Earth, was from the same Earth that I had cursed after the fall. I accepted Abel's offering and rejected Cain's gift. All of the false religions of this world which are, in reality, following the belief system of Cain will have the same conclusion—rejection. They will be valueless."[35]

"I remember the two brothers," said Becky. "I see now

35. Genesis 4:1–16; Hebrews 11:4.

that there is a deep, underlying meaning to the story. There is a very important reason why one gift was accepted and the other rejected. Abel did it *Your way*. Cain did it *his way*. I always thought it was just the story of sibling rivalry," Becky said.

Jesus replied, "The stories in the Bible are wrapped in truths. Sometimes, one truth is overlaid over another. It is a gold mine with golden nuggets waiting to be discovered." Becky's eyes opened wide with excitement![36]

"Do you remember the Passover story, Becky?" Jesus asked.

Becky replied, "Yes, we observe Passover in my house every year. It's a wonderful story, but my father sits at the head of the table and reads every single word of the Haggadah out loud. It takes forever! The delicious food is on the table, and he just sits there and reads and reads. He goes on and on while we are all starving!"

Jesus smiled. "It is very good that your family observes Passover because there is a very deep connection between the blood which was applied on the doorposts that night

36. Proverbs 25:2; Deuteronomy 29:2.

and My crucifixion. As you know, the story of Passover describes how I delivered the Israelites from their bondage in Egypt using ten spectacular miracles. Moses told them to place the blood of the lamb on the doorposts of their hastily prepared shacks. He told them if they obeyed, I would protect them. When the angel of death passed over their homes that night, I would see the blood, and death would *pass over* them. Moses did not say, 'Put a list of your good works on the door, and God will recognize your good works, and you will be kept safe.' No, it was the blood of the lamb and their obedience to My instruction which kept them from death.[37]

"In the same way, when someone accepts Me as their Savior by faith, the blood that I shed on the cross is placed on their hearts [metaphorically], and when their appointed time of death arrives, God's judgment will pass over them. The lamb that was slain in the wilderness that night was a shadow of what was to come later in its fullness. You see, Becky, that lamb was pointing to Me. I am the Lamb of God. Everyone who believes in Me will pass through the

---

37. 1 Corinthians 5:7.

dark valley of death, as if it was a shadow, and will emerge on the other side where I will be waiting for them to take them to My Father's house. My Father is like the father in the biblical story of the prodigal son. Like a parent, He is patiently waiting for the return of the Jewish people and the rest of His lost creation. When the prodigal son's father spotted his son at a distance, he ran to greet him. The reason he spotted him so quickly is because he was always looking for him. Whenever he was in the field or walking on the road, he always glanced at the horizon in the hopes he would someday see him returning home. And when he finally did see him, he was so happy. His son who had left home had returned. That is how My Father will greet the Jewish people when they return home. With tears in His eyes and joy in His heart, He will embrace them. They will return in large numbers, someday, but it will take time.[38] Be assured, it will definitely happen according to My Father's timetable. The clock is ticking Becky."

Becky, surprised, said, "I don't think the Jewish people know this, do they?"

---

38. Revelation 12:11.

Jesus said, "Some do, but most do not. I am going to give you some Scripture verses to read. In this way, you will see the whole story unfold, and you will see Me clearly in the Jewish Scriptures."

"How will I see You?" she said.

"You will see Me because I will open your eyes. I have to leave now, but I'll return." And with those words, the swirl of radiant colors faded together with Him, and He was gone.

Becky heard her mother calling her to breakfast, and she hurried downstairs. Breakfast was a solemn affair. Her grandmother had gone home, and Charlie had left for baseball practice. Only her mother and father were seated at the table. Her father said, "Becky, your mother and I are very unhappy about what happened last night. Grandma was very upset about this Jesus thing and left early this morning. She didn't want to see you. We are all hoping that this is only a phase you are going through and will soon come to an end. We are Jews, and Jews don't believe in or even talk about Jesus."

Becky's mother interrupted and added, "Becky, please consider what you are doing. You can't be serious about this. Don't disgrace our family."

Becky could hardly swallow her oatmeal. It just stuck in her throat. However, she did manage to speak. "But you don't really know Him. Look, I don't know why this is happening to me, but it is happening. I tell you, He's real." She took a few mouthfuls of oatmeal and left the table.

CHAPTER 4

Becky ran up the stairs and dressed. Because it was Saturday, she returned to her favorite place—the esplanade by the sea—taking her Bible with her. She found her favorite spot and sat down. As she listened to the familiar sound of the waves gently washing against the jetty rocks, she thought about the events of the past few days. *Boy, this is some experience*, she thought. *And it sure has upset a lot of people!*

She opened her Bible and began to read the book of Matthew in the Newer Testament. This time, she thought,

I will read it more slowly. With the book open in her lap, she remembered that Jesus had told her to begin studying the Newer Testament, reading the book of Matthew. He told her that Matthew was a Jewish tax collector, a disciple of His, and he was writing to Jewish people. Jesus said, "The Jewish tax collectors were treated as outcasts by the Jewish community because they were perceived as working for Rome and, therefore, turning their backs on Our people. Some were even considered spies. One day, I passed by, saw Matthew, and called out to him saying, 'Follow Me.' Matthew was one of the last persons the people thought that I would have chosen to follow Me. To follow 'in the steps of a Rabbi' was a distinct honor. Always remember, Becky, My ways and thoughts are not the same as the world thinks" (Isaiah 58:8–9, NIV).

As Becky read the pages, she noticed that every so often, Matthew would make a reference to an Older Testament Scripture verse. He would describe a scene in Jesus's life and then write, "As it was spoken by the prophets." As she continued reading, she recognized that every once in a while, he would describe some of the narrative of Jesus's life and then refer to the prophets.

This phrase, "as it was spoken by the prophets," became a drum beat in her mind. "As it was spoken by the prophets, as it was spoken by the prophets, as it was spoken by the prophets." Becky wondered as she read, *What was spoken, and where can I find it?* Then, suddenly, she noticed that in the margin of some pages, there were references to Older Testament Scripture verses. As Becky was reading Matthew's writings, a pattern emerged. She read a passage in Matthew and then turned back to read the Older Testament Scripture verse to which Matthew was pointing. The newer and older verses, although written many, many years apart, seemed remarkably similar. It was as if the writer in the Older Testament knew ahead of time what was going to happen in the future. Becky found this very intriguing, and she read through the whole book of Matthew, underlining the relevant passages and matching them with the prophecies in the Older Testament.

There were several verses which caught her eye. She read in the Older Testament: "…A star shall come out of Jacob, and a scepter shall rise out of Israel" (Numbers 24:17, ESV).

Becky mulled over the words "star" and "scepter" and thought, *Who holds a scepter? A king does!*

Then, she read in the Newer Testament: "Now after Jesus was born in Bethlehem of Judea in the days of Herod the king, behold, wise men came from the east came to Jerusalem, saying, 'Where is He who has been born King of the Jews? For we saw His star when it rose and have come to worship Him'" (Matthew 2:1–2, ESV). Then, she read two other Scripture verses, one in the Older Testament and another in the Newer Testament: "But you, Bethlehem Ephratah…out of you will come for Me One who will be ruler over Israel" (Micah 5:2 NIV).

"…Jesus was born in Bethlehem of Judea" (Matthew 2:1, ESV).

"Mmm, Jesus was born in Bethlehem," murmured Becky to herself. *This is very interesting,* Becky thought.

How did the writers in the Older Testament know about future events? Were they fortune tellers? No, she read that they were called prophets. She learned that God told them what was going to happen ahead of time so that the Jewish people would be able to identify the Messiah when He came. She began searching for the Scripture verses Jesus gave her before He left that morning.

Becky sat there for quite some time going back-and-forth between the Newer and Older Testaments, and slowly, she began to see that some of the verses in the Older Testament were describing many of the events in Jesus's life which happened many, many years later.

As she sat there, reading, the steady rhythm of the waves sounded far away like background music, and she felt she had entered another dimension—a timeless one. Slowly, she began to connect the dots of the prophetic Scripture verses and a face began to emerge. "I know who this is!" she said out loud. "It's Jesus." As if speaking to an unseen person, she added, "What is Jesus doing in the Older Testament? How come they didn't see it? It's all there.

Jesus is the promised Messiah!"

Then, she remembered that Jesus had told her that Satan had blinded the eyes of the Jewish people, as well as most of the whole world, so they couldn't see. He said, "He doesn't want anyone to come to Me and be saved." She remembered that Jesus had told her that the invitation to be saved had been extended to the Gentiles as well.

She asked Jesus why Satan hated the Jews in particular. "He hates the Jewish people almost as much as he hates Me. I am his archenemy because God's promised Messiah, a Jew, came through them. When you get to the end of the Bible, Becky, and read the book of Revelation, you will see that he is, eventually, defeated by Me. He knows this, and that is one of the reasons he has been attacking the Jewish people from the very beginning. Time and time again, he tried to cut off their line, so I wouldn't be born.[39]

"Having failed in that attempt, he continued attacking them and is still attacking them, using all kinds of strategies—mostly lies. All of the anti-Semitism they have experienced and are still experiencing is orchestrated

39. Revelation 12:1–6; Matthew 2:16–18.

by Satan. It has its roots in his hatred of Me. He knows that in the end, he will be totally vanquished by Me, but he is in denial of the truth. The web of lies he spins around others has engulfed him." Becky remembered their conversation as she sat on the rocks looking up at the clouds.[40]

Becky was excited and surprised about what she just read in the Scriptures, but she was also worried. "What am I going to do? I can't talk to my family, and even some of my friends are upset with me. Who can I talk to? I know, I'll go and speak to Rabbi Bernard. He knows me and my family very well."

A loud splash startled Becky. She had almost forgotten where she was. A big fish had jumped out of the water. As she watched him swimming around, she thought with a little envy, that fish has such a nice, simple life! Then, Becky jumped off the rocks and headed for the Jewish temple which was nearby. As she walked, a Scripture verse came to her mind, "I will put salvation in Zion, for Israel my glory" (Isaiah 46:13, ESV).

Jesus was born in Israel, Becky thought.

---

40. Exodus 1:8–10, 15–16; Esther 3:5–6.

CHAPTER 5

Entering the temple, she immediately went to the sanctuary and sat down on one of the pews. She needed to collect her thoughts. "What am I going to say to Rabbi Bernard?"

The sanctuary was beautiful. The soft lighting revealed the beautiful symbols of her Jewish faith. On a table, she saw a large, golden menorah, then, she looked up and admired the familiar white sculptured Stars of David embossed on the dark-blue paneling which circled the whole room, just below the ceiling. As she looked around the room, she saw the bema in front of the sanctuary and the curtains which hid the sacred Torah. It was a familiar setting. She had spent a lot of time in that sanctuary studying Hebrew in preparation for her Bat Mitzvah several years ago.

She heard a noise in the hallway which interrupted her thoughts, and she left the sanctuary in search of Rabbi Bernard. She found him in his office. He immediately recognized Becky and welcomed her into his office. "Hi, Becky, it's so nice to see you. It's been a long time," he said.

Sheepishly, she replied, "I know, I've been very busy at school."

He invited her to sit down and asked her why she had come to see him. Becky told him the whole story of her encounter with Jesus.

The rabbi listened intently to everything she was saying, his eyes fixed on her face. When she finished speaking, he said, "Becky, I have known you and your family for a very long time. You know I am always straightforward and direct. This is not a good story. I think I know you well enough to ask you a pointed question. Are you taking any kind of medication or drugs? I know this, sometimes, occurs among young people. Please be honest with me. I am very concerned."

"No, rabbi," Becky replied, "I am not taking any drugs. Everything I told you actually happened. This is the second time someone has mentioned drugs. Why is it that when something unusual happens, people think that it is related to drugs? You always spoke about life being so much more than our finite minds can comprehend. And you often told us that God moves in mysterious ways."

"Becky," the rabbi said, "you are a young Jewish girl. Why would Jesus who lived and died two thousand years ago come to you in a vision? Although many people think He is God, He was only a man."

"But that's just the point," Becky replied, "maybe He isn't just an ordinary person. Maybe, He is the Messiah, and we made a terrible mistake. Did you know that He was a Rabbi? I didn't know that. And He told a woman He met at a well that He was the Messiah. Now, why would He do that? Either He was crazy, lying, or He was telling the truth. You know, I've been skimming through the whole Bible, the Older and Newer Testaments, and there are over three hundred predictions in the Older Testament that match the story of Jesus's life. How do you explain that? They can't all be coincidences. No, I am beginning to believe that He really is the promised Messiah."

The rabbi replied, "Becky, in your life's journey, you will meet many people who believe different things. We are Jews and have a very rich spiritual and cultural heritage. Jews don't believe in Jesus. I see that you are really very serious and are searching for answers to some deep questions regarding the meaning of life and your identity as a Jew. You are turning to the Bible for those answers, and that's a good thing because there is much wisdom written there. However, I don't think you will find all of your answers there.

"Becky, being Jewish is so much more than just what the Bible says it is. Judaism is a deeply rich spiritual culture whose roots go back for thousands of years. As Jews, we have a strong, unshakeable bond. One of the strongest bonds between people is one that has been forged by suffering. As you know, as Jews we have suffered so much persecution. There were the inquisitions, the crusades, and the Holocaust. That—combined with our loyalty to 'tradition' and love of the land of Israel—binds us together and gives us hope for the future. Becky, I have known you and your family for a long time, and I am very fond of all of you. I will pray for you. You are on the wrong road. One that will only lead to heartache for you and your family. If you give up being a Jew, you will regret it for the rest of your life."

Becky, deeply disturbed by the rabbi's response, said, "There is something I just don't understand. My friend, Barbara, practices yoga, has a guru, and is still considered Jewish. My Uncle Sol doesn't ever go to temple, not even on the high holy days, and he's considered Jewish. And someone can be an atheist and still be considered a Jew. But if I follow a Rabbi descended from King David who makes a credible claim to be the Messiah of Israel, somehow, I'm not Jewish? Can you please explain that to me?"

Rabbi Bernard took a deep breath, paused a moment

to think, and then said in a deeply compassionate tone, "Becky, Becky, how did you get into this muddle? All I can do is to tell you that I will get down on my knees tonight and pray for you."

Feeling sad and disappointed, Becky, left his office and returned to the temple sanctuary. She knelt down and prayed, with tears streaming down her face, "Oh, God, please help me. I don't know what to do. No one understands me anymore." She stayed in the sanctuary a while, absorbing the peaceful silence into her troubled soul.

Becky realized that something had changed. She didn't feel the same way she used to feel when she was in the temple sanctuary. It wasn't the years that had passed since she was in Hebrew school. It was her experience with Jesus that had changed everything.

She said to herself, "Something is missing here." It was almost as if she could see Jesus standing in the doorway with a very sad expression on His face which said, *I am not welcome here.* On the pew, a few rows in front of her, she noticed an open Bible and a prayer shawl. She thought,

Jesus probably wore a prayer shawl just like that one.

When she saw the prayer shawl, she remembered something. It happened during a Friday-night service several years ago in that very sanctuary. Men were being called up one by one to read from the Torah. One man, in particular, approached the podium and read a portion of the Scriptures. He was wearing the traditional yarmulke on his head, and a prayer shawl was wrapped around his shoulders. When he finished reading, he slowly bent down and very reverently kissed the page. *That was such a beautiful moment, one I will never forget*, Becky thought.

After a while, she arose and left the temple. As she walked toward her home, she was deeply absorbed in her thoughts. She saw her house in the distance and felt a little fearful. She remembered the tension-filled breakfast that morning. Reaching her house, she took a deep breath and opened the front door. Very quickly, she determined that no one was home. With a sigh of relief, she headed for the kitchen. She was hungry, so she quickly made a salad for lunch, then, went upstairs and took a nap.

After a few hours of restful sleep, she awoke. The rays of the setting sun streaming through her window created a beautiful glow in her room. Then, she saw the familiar swirl of many colors and Jesus in the midst of them.

He looked at Becky compassionately and said, "Becky, don't be upset. Rabbi Bernard is a very fine man, and he means well, but he is not seeing things clearly. You won't be able to change his mind either. Only I can. There is something I would like you to do.[41] Tomorrow is Sunday. There is a church nearby. They have an adjacent theatre and are presenting a play entitled 'The Tribunal.' I think you will enjoy it, and I encourage you to go. Why don't you call Barbara and make plans to attend?"

Becky replied, "Okay, that sounds good. I need a distraction now."

Jesus smiled and said, "I don't know how much of a distraction it will be, but it will be very helpful to you. Becky, you are on a spiritual journey now. Think of it as an adventure. Be strong and courageous. You can trust Me and My love for you." With those words, Jesus and the

41. Proverbs 20:12.

colorful circle quickly faded, and He was gone.

Becky picked up the phone, called Barbara, and filled her in on all that had recently transpired. Barbara was excited and said, "I hope you are writing all of this down in a journal. You really should, you know." They talked some more, then made plans to attend the performance the next day.

CHAPTER 6

Sunday was a beautiful day. Becky and Barbara met in front of the theatre at 1:00 p.m. They bought their tickets, entered the theatre, and sat down. The church annex had been transformed into a theatre. The stage up front was hidden by a heavy maroon curtain. Klieg lights hung from the ceiling. Barbara handed Becky the program and said, "Let's read it."

Becky opened to the first page. There was a brief description about the play. It read, "After the crucifixion of Jesus, the Roman senate was greatly disturbed about the news coming from Judea. It seems there was a great deal of unrest among the people there. There were reports of sightings of a so-called 'risen Jesus.' People were arguing and fighting in the streets, and most disturbing of all, some were calling Him a King. The Roman senate called a special meeting and discussed the matter. Since Emperor Tiberius was considered the only king at that time and Judea was subject to Roman rule, they decided to send some Roman senators to Jerusalem to find out what was going on. They held a meeting in Pontius Pilate's palace and convened a secret tribunal whose purpose was to interview some people who had witnessed some of the recent events. This tribunal is not recorded in history, but not everything that happened in Judea at that time was reported."

Becky looked around at the audience. The theatre was crowded, and people were chatting. Suddenly, the lights began to dim, and the noise level diminished, and then, there was silence in hushed anticipation. A minute or two later, the hanging curtain slowly rose to reveal a large room in Pontius Pilate's palace. It was a beautifully decorated room befitting a man of his prominence. Seated at a marble rectangular table in the middle of the room were three Roman senators dressed in white togas bearing the emblems of Rome. The table was at an angle, and in front of the table, was a single chair.

One of the senators spoke to the other two men and said, "I think we are ready to begin. We've assembled a good amount of witnesses who will tell us what we want to know. Let's begin."

One of the senators rang a loud bell which was on the table, and after a minute or two passed, a woman was ushered into the room.

She looked apprehensive, and the same senator said to her, "There is no need to be afraid. This is not a trial. We are here only to gather information. We understand that you knew this man called Jesus. Is that true?"

She began by saying, "Yes, my name is Martha. I am the sister of Mary and Lazarus. Jesus was a friend of ours. He often stayed with us in our house to rest and refresh Himself after His travels up and down the countryside. One day, when Jesus was away on one of His trips, my brother, Lazarus, fell very ill. He was close to death. Mary and I sent word to Jesus to come quickly. We knew of His power to heal people. We had seen Him to do it many times.

"He healed a blind man, a man with a withered hand, and He even cast out demons from people. But to our surprise, Jesus did not return right away. In fact, even though He was not very far away, He didn't return for several days. Mary and I did not understand this. I was very angry. He was supposed to be our friend. He had healed others—strangers. Why didn't He come to us? Well, our brother Lazarus died. Mary and I were devastated. We wrapped him in burial clothes and buried him in one of our family tombs. To be frank, I was very disappointed in Jesus. I felt He had failed us. Several days after Lazarus died, I was looking out of my window, and I saw Jesus and a few of His disciples coming toward our house. *Now He comes*, I thought as I ran to meet Him.

"When I met Him, I asked Him why He didn't come sooner. I was crying. He looked at me and some of the people in our garden who had come to comfort us, and He began to weep too.

"He turned to me and said, 'Martha, your brother will rise again.' He had told me He was the resurrection and the life and all who believed in Him, even though they would die, would live again. He asked me if I believed that and I told Him that I did, adding that I believed He was the Christ—the promised Messiah we were waiting for. Then, He asked all of us to follow Him to Lazarus's tomb. We all wondered why. What was He going to do? Then, Jesus asked us to remove the stone which was in front of the tomb. I told Him that Lazarus had been dead for four days, and his body probably had begun to decompose.[42]

"Then, Jesus turned to me and said, 'Did I not tell you that if you would believe, you would see the glory of God?' So we removed the stone. Then, Jesus lifted up His eyes to heaven, prayed, and said, 'Father, I thank You that You have heard Me.' When He said this, He shouted with a loud voice, 'Lazarus, come out!' We were all amazed and took a step backward. We didn't know what to expect.

42. John 11:1–44.

"A few minutes passed, and we saw the figure of a man slowly walk out of the tomb. He was wrapped in linen cloths. Even his face was covered with a burial cloth. Jesus told us to unwrap him. We did so, and I couldn't believe my eyes. It was Lazarus. He was alive! Everyone was astonished and overjoyed. Our friends who were there that day began to talk among themselves. They were saying, 'Jesus must be the Messiah. Only the Messiah could do something like this.' It was something no one had ever seen before!

"We all returned to our house with Lazarus and had a party that afternoon. What a party that was! Jesus and the disciples stayed with us, and we all rejoiced. My brother who was dead was now alive! As I fell asleep that night, I reviewed the events of the day in my mind. I couldn't stop thinking about it. Then, I understood why Jesus didn't come to us right away.

"Yes, He had the power to heal Lazarus who was sick, but His plan was to do something greater. He planned to raise Lazarus from the dead! What a day that was—one I will never forget. My brother is now home with us, and every once in a while, I must confess, I touch him on his arm just to make sure it is really him. With your permission, I would like to say something."

The senators, who had been listening to her story intently, nodded their heads and said, "Yes, go ahead."

Martha thanked them and said, "I don't know why Jesus was crucified. He never hurt anyone. All He ever did was heal and help people."

One of the senators asked her, "Do you think it is possible that your brother wasn't really dead when he was placed in the tomb?"

Martha replied, "No, he was definitely dead. He had no pulse, and my sister, Mary, and I were the ones who wrapped him in the burial clothes. He was in the tomb for four days. The stone was tightly fitted into the entrance of the tomb. No, it's not possible he was alive."

One of the other senators asked her if Jesus considered Himself to be a king. Martha said, "Oh no, He would never think of Himself that way. He was humble, kind, and thought of Himself as a servant. On one occasion,

He took a towel, put it around His waist, and washed His disciples' feet."

The senators thanked her, and she left the room.

One of the senators said, "What an amazing story. Who was this man they called Jesus?" The other two senators didn't reply.

Another senator rang the bell, and the second witness was brought into the room. She was an extremely old woman. She walked very slowly with a cane and was invited to take a seat and asked to state her name.

She said, "My name is Elizabeth. I am a very, very old woman now, but my eyes have beheld wondrous things. I was told you were sent from Rome to find out what is going on here. In order to understand what is going on now, we need to go back to the very beginning. I was there when it all began.

"It started with my husband, Zachariah, who served as a priest in the temple. He received a visit from the Angel Gabriel who told my husband that even though I was getting on in years, I would soon become pregnant and bear a son, and he told him to name him John. He said that our son would be great in the eyes of the Lord, and he would prepare the way for the coming of the Messiah of Israel.

"I did become pregnant and gave birth to a son, and we named him John. We could see that God's calling was clearly on his life. Filled with God's Holy Spirit from his birth, he lived in the desert and baptized many, turning them back to our God—the God of Israel.

"I was a relative of Mary, the mother of Jesus. During the sixth month of my pregnancy with John, Jesus's mother came to visit me. She told me that she, too, was visited by the Angel Gabriel, and he told her that she also would give birth to a Son. Only her story was more remarkable than mine. The angel told her that God's Holy Spirit would come upon her and that her Son would be great and be called the Son of the Most High. Mary was very surprised because she was engaged but not yet married to Joseph, and they had not been intimate. But Mary believed the angel and accepted the will of God for her life. One of the amazing things that happened was that when Mary first appeared at my door, at the sound of her voice, the baby in my womb leaped for joy. I actually felt the baby jump! This was only the beginning of many amazing things that followed.

"Mary stayed with me for three months until I gave birth. We talked about many things, especially about our unborn babies. We wondered about God's plan for their lives, especially with two separate visits from the Angel Gabriel telling us that both of our babies had God's favor on their lives.

"We were very excited. And then, we found two Jewish Scripture verses. One said, 'A voice of one calling: In the desert prepare the way for the Lord; make straight in the wilderness a highway for our God' [Isaiah 40:3, NIV]. I said to Mary, 'That's what Gabriel told my husband about my baby.'

"Then, we found another Jewish Scripture which said, 'Therefore the Lord Himself will give you a sign: the virgin will conceive and give birth to a son' [Isaiah 7:14, NIV].

Mary said, 'That must be me, and my baby will be the promised Messiah!'

"We were both speechless. We knew that the Jewish prophet Isaiah lived about seven hundred years before us, so this was truly remarkable. When we read these verses, we held hands, bowed our heads, and prayed. We prayed for both of our babies and the plan that God had for them."

One of the Senators said, "We heard that your son, John, was beheaded by Herod, and Jesus was crucified. It doesn't sound like your God had a very good plan for them!"

"I believe it was a glorious plan," Elizabeth replied. "John's purpose was to preach a message of repentance and to prepare the way of the Messiah who was Jesus. Jesus's purpose was to die a sacrificial death on the cross for the sins of the whole world. Our God's purpose for them was fulfilled just as He had told us in the Jewish Scriptures."

The third senator leaned over the table. "You believe in these Scriptures of yours, don't you? They carry a lot of weight."

"Yes, we believe they are written by God's Holy Spirit and that He breathed His life into the very words themselves."

"How is that possible?"

"Well, He created everything there is in the whole universe, so I imagine it is not too difficult to breathe His life into the words of a book."

The first senator probed further. "Did the followers of Jesus consider Him a King when He was alive, and do they consider Him a King today? We know how a legend can become very powerful over time. That's the main reason we are here. We want to squash any seditious acts before they occur. Tiberius is king and the only king."

Elizabeth said, "Some of His followers wanted Jesus to become a strong political leader, but He was not interested in that. His life had a different purpose. His kingdom, He said, was not of this world. He told us that His power and authority came from a different place."

"Where is this place?"

"The only thing I can tell you with certainty is that He came from that place, and when His work was completed, He returned to that place. And that is where He is now, waiting for us who believe in Him." She smiled at the thought.

The senator who had remained silent throughout the questioning of Elizabeth said, "I have one final question. How were you able to accept the idea of a virgin birth? Being pregnant yourself, you weren't ignorant about how a baby is born."

Elizabeth replied, "To be honest, in the back of my mind, I always wondered about that. So when Jesus was an adult, I asked Him. He reminded me that with God, all things are possible. Jesus said He had created the natural laws, and He could suspend them at will. He also told me why a virgin birth was necessary."

The three senators leaned forward in their chairs. She had their complete and undivided attention.

Elizabeth continued, "Jesus told me that the whole human race is born with the legacy of Adam and the consequences of the fall. A human being could not atone for the sins of the world. A mere mortal is born spiritually dead, separated from God, and under His curse. Because of this, He could not be God's effective instrument for such an event. It would take an act of God. He Himself would have to be the sin bearer and, therefore, it required an "immaculate conception" to birth the Son of God."

The three senators looked at each other. Finally, one of them said, "Thank you, Elizabeth, for the information you have shared with us." He rang the bell. One of Pilate's officials entered the room and gently escorted her out.

At the tables, the senators shuffled some papers, briefly whispered something inaudible to each other, and waited for the next witness. The door opened, and another woman walked in and sat down in the appointed chair. They repeated the same opening remarks and asked her to share her story.

She began by saying, "I knew this man called Jesus. I met Him one day at a well. I am from Samaria, and at the time I met Him, I was considered an outcast in my community mainly because I had had many husbands, and the man I was living with was not my husband. So on the day we met, I was going to the well for water as I usually did each day, around noon. I always chose that time of the day, so I wouldn't have to meet anyone from my town. They were very critical of me. When I came to the well, a man was sitting there. I could see that He was Jewish because He was wearing a Jewish prayer shawl.

"Quite to my surprise, He spoke to me. Jewish men usually don't speak to women and especially someone from Samaria. He asked me for a drink of water, and we began to talk. He seemed very nice, and He told me He had living water to give me. I looked for His bucket, but I didn't see one, so I asked Him where He was going to get this water. He told me that everyone who drank the water from the well I was drinking from would thirst again, but everyone who drank from the water He would give me would never thirst again. I really didn't understand what He meant.

"If He gave me the water He was talking about. *I wouldn't have to come to the well every day*, I thought.

"But He explained that the water He was talking about was very different. It would become a spring of water which would continually flow in me. He asked me to go and call my husband. I told Him that I didn't have a husband. Then, He told me a remarkable thing. He said I answered truthfully for He knew that the man I was living with was not my husband, and He reminded me that I have had five husbands. I was shocked that He knew so much about me. I had never met Him before.

"We talked some more about religious matters, and I began to suspect He was a prophet of some kind. I told Him that I had heard that a Messiah—the Anointed One—was coming soon and that He would tell us everything that we needed to know. He looked directly in my eyes and said, 'I who speak to you am He' [John 4:26, ESV]. That remark took my breath away. He spoke with such confidence and authority. It was such a matter-of-fact statement, as if He were telling me, 'Look up at the sky, see, the sun is shining today.' I was so taken aback by what He said that I dropped my water pot.

"In the distance, I could see some men approaching the well. When they came near, they began to speak to

Him, and I could tell they were some of His friends. I felt uncomfortable with all of the men, so I said goodbye and returned to my hometown which was nearby.

"I told the people in my town all about the conversation I had with Jesus and told them that He must be the Messiah, the one we had heard about, because He told me so many things about myself. They were so impressed that they rushed to the well to meet Him. They asked Him to stay with us for a few days which He did. During that time, we all talked about many things, and many believed that He really was the promised Messiah.

"After these events, the people in town treated me differently. They were more respectful and friendly toward me. It was truly amazing. Because of this man, everything changed for me. I felt that I now belonged. I regret only one thing. I never thanked Him for what He did for me. And as I think back, I am convinced that He knew I would be coming to the well at the exact hour I arrived. Actually, I believe He was waiting for me. We had an unscheduled appointment."

One of the senators asked her, "So He definitely told you He was this Messiah?"

The woman replied, "Yes. That is exactly what He said."

Becky turned to Barbara and, in a loud voice, said, "See, I told you."

The people sitting around her turned and said, "Shhh! Be quiet!"

The second senator asked the woman how she knew about a Messiah since she was from Samaria. He also asked her why she believed Jesus whom she said was a stranger.

The woman said, "We had heard rumors for a long time about a prophet—a Messiah who would be coming and would perform great and unusual things. I believed Jesus because He seemed very different from other men. He seemed very calm, confident, and peaceful. He knew all about my life, and He spoke to me in a manner in which no man ever spoke to me. It was as if He was speaking to the deepest part of me—my soul."

The senators thanked the woman for her cooperation,

and she departed.

One of the senators said, "Well, it seems that a lot went on here in Judea while we were in Rome, but the fact is that Jesus was only a man, and He is dead. It's true that He seems to have impacted the lives of the people He came in contact with, but I don't think it will have any lasting effect."

"I don't think so either."

The lights on stage began to dim, and the curtain slowly descended. The lights in the theatre came up for intermission.

CHAPTER 7

Becky and Barbara got up from their seats to stretch their legs. As they walked to the theatre lobby, which was filling up with people, Becky said, "Well, what do you think? Those were some stories! I especially liked Elizabeth's story. I had never heard about her before."

Barbara, deep in thought, finally answered, "I never heard any of these stories before. I only read the story of creation in the first part of the Torah, but now, I think I will read the whole Bible—the Older and the Newer Testaments."

Becky said, "When I was in Hebrew school, we only read the Older Testament. The other day, I borrowed the whole Bible from the library, and now, I am reading both the Older and Newer Testaments. Jesus told me it is really just one book and has one Author—Himself. He is the storyteller.[43]

"He said His story begins in Genesis—the first book of the Torah—when mankind lost everything he had in the garden. The story ends in a book called Revelation which is at the end of the Newer Testament. Everything is restored. He said it is one book, different stories, but one major theme runs throughout—God's plan of redemption."

The two girls talked some more and meandered around the theatre lobby until the lights flickered, signaling that intermission was over. They returned to their seats as the lights began to dim. The curtain rose, and the second act began. The setting was the same. The three Roman senators were seated at the large table, and an empty chair was in front of them.

One of the senators rang the now familiar bell, and one of Governor Pilate's officials ushered in an elderly man. He carried himself with dignity and quietly sat down. Once

43. Luke 24:25–27.

again, one of the senators told the man that this was not a trial. He said they were sent from Rome to gather facts about some very unusual things happening in Judea.

"We have already spoken to Governor Pilate who filled us in on some of the facts, but we want to hear from you," one of them said. Then, the man was asked to state his name.

He began by saying, "My name is Gamaliel. I am a Pharisee and a member of the Sanhedrin, the ruling body of the religious Jewish community. I am also the grandson of Hillel."

One of the senators asked him, "Who is Hillel?"

Gamaliel responded, "He was a rabbi and considered a great teacher by my people—the Jews."

"Please go on," said the senator.

Gamaliel continued, "This man called Jesus and His disciples presented a very grave problem to us. Even now, after His death, we are trying to grapple with it. He had a tremendous influence on many people here because of His teaching and the miracles He performed. Some people called Him a wonder worker. Just recently, some of His disciples were brought before our council and told not to continue teaching in His name. At one point, the exchange between the disciples and the council became very heated, and I stood up and warned the council not to take any drastic action against these men. I reminded them that several times before, some men had claimed to be the Messiah and also drew large crowds of followers, but they passed from the scene and are gone. I told the council to leave the disciples alone and warned them that if this movement was of human origin, it would come to nothing. But if it was of God, they would not be able to stop, overthrow, or destroy it. I added that they might even find themselves to be fighting God, and that is very dangerous."

The first senator spoke, "You saw and heard this man called Jesus. Can you tell us something about Him?"

Gamaliel went on. "He was very different from most men. He had a presence about Him and spoke with great authority, but it appeared to me that He didn't really want us to understand what He was saying because He never answered any of our questions directly. His replies were oblique, hidden in mystery. This infuriated some of our council members."[44]

The second senator asked Gamaliel, "Do you think He was this Messiah whom people spoke about?"

Gamaliel replied, "I don't know. Sometimes, I wake up in the middle of the night and worry about what happened. The events leading up to His crucifixion occurred so fast."

"We heard reports that some people have seen Him after the crucifixion. Have you seen Him?"

Gamaliel replied, "No, I haven't, but I, too, have heard about these reports, and it confirms my deepest fear."

"And what is that?" asked the Senator.

"That a terrible mistake was made." He paused for a moment, deep in thought. Then, he continued, "There is something else that haunts me. My grandfather, Hillel, often taught, 'What is hateful to you, do not do to your neighbor. That is the whole Torah. The rest is

44. Matthew 7:29; Mark 1:22.

the explanation of this—go and study it.'[45] After the crucifixion of Jesus, one of His followers came to me and asked me why Jesus was crucified. I told him that Jesus claimed to be God which was blasphemy in violation of Moses's law, and He claimed to be a king which was a violation of Roman law. It was perceived by our leaders that His claims put us in a dangerous position with our God and with the Roman authorities.

"Then, this man told me that Jesus often taught, 'Do to others as you would have them do to you' [Luke 6:31, NIV]. I never heard Jesus actually say that, but others did. The thought came to me. Perhaps, when He was a young boy, He heard my grandfather teaching in the temple. When Jesus was young, He was often seen in the temple talking to the elders. So he may have been quoting my grandfather whom I loved so dearly. If that is true, I didn't know that at the time of Jesus's trial." Gamaliel's eyes began to fill with tears.[46]

The senators looked at each other and awkwardly thanked Gamaliel for his testimony, then, one of them rang

---

45. From the Talmud, tractate Shabbat 31a.
46. Luke 2:41–52.

the bell. Gamaliel slowly rose from the chair and walked toward the door.

The next witness who entered was a young boy. He walked hesitantly toward the chair and appeared to be afraid. The third senator told him not to be fearful. "We are only here to gather information. We heard that you were present when this man called Jesus performed one of His miracles. Can you tell us about it?"

The boy trembled slightly. "Am I in in trouble? I am the one who gave him the food which was in the basket."

"You are not in any trouble. Just tell us the whole story."

Forgetting his fear, he became excited as he recalled his meeting with the rabbi. "I remember I was looking out of my window and saw some people walking on the road. One of the men who passed by saw me and yelled, 'Come with us, the rabbi is teaching.' As I was leaving, my mother gave me a basket for lunch. In it were two small fish and five barley loaves, so I would have something to eat and, maybe, share with someone else. I followed the people, and when we arrived at a hill, everyone was already seated. The Rabbi was speaking, and being small, I was able to move up close to Him. I thought He might be hungry, so I offered Him my basket of food. He smiled and thanked me.

"I sat down next to Him, thinking He was going to take some food for Himself and then give me back my basket. But He didn't do that. Instead, He took the basket and, looking up toward the sky, said, 'Thank You.' Then, He gave the basket to His friends who took some food and passed the basket around to the people who were seated on the grass. Suddenly, from out of nowhere, more baskets with fish and barley appeared. I was so surprised because I had only brought one basket with two small fish and five barley loaves from home. Now, there were many baskets filled with fish and barley loaves, and all the people were being fed. There were so many people on the hill that day. I couldn't believe my eyes! I ate the portion that was handed to me and looked at the Rabbi. He looked at me and smiled. After all the people ate, there were twelve baskets full of leftover food. I jumped up and looked into the baskets, and they were filled with the broken pieces of barley loaves and fishes. I remember thinking He must be a magician. I sat down and just looked at Him. He looked at me again and just smiled.

"The sun was beginning to set so the people folded up their blankets and began to leave. The people were talking about the food and calling it a miracle. I joined the crowd and headed back home carrying the original basket I had brought. It contained some of the fish and barley loaves. I kept looking into the basket counting the pieces. I heard some people call Him a miracle worker. Some of them asked me several times what was in the basket I had given to the Rabbi.

"I told them, 'Only two small fish and five barley loaves.'

"A few people laughed and said, 'If that was all you brought, how could He feed that many people?'

"I told them, 'I don't know, but I am sure of what was in my basket when I left home that day.'"

The senator raised an eyebrow. "Thank you for your

story. Did you ever see Him do something like that before?"

"No, I didn't, but I sure wish I had. I will never forget that day or Him. Do you know why He was killed? He was such a nice man."

"No, son, it's very complicated," the senator gently replied.

"My parents always say that about everything." The boy frowned.

The senators smiled at each other, and then, one of them rang the bell. The young boy jumped off the chair, and Pilate's official escorted him out the door.

Another witness entered the room, walked over to the chair, and sat down. He said, "My name is Barabbas, and I met Jesus during the feast of Passover. I was in jail because I was a criminal. I had done some very bad things. It is customary at that time of year to pardon one prisoner. Two of us were selected—Jesus and me. Both of us were brought before the crowd in the palace courtyard and presented to the crowd. Governor Pontius Pilate asked them to choose between the two of us. The crowd shouted both of our names for a while, but finally, the sound of my name was heard above that of Jesus's name. So I was the one they set free.[47]

"I've had a hard time understanding why I was chosen. I was a criminal and deserved to be in jail. As a result of what happened, my life changed in a big way. It changed because the man called Jesus died instead of me.

"After He was sentenced to be crucified, I followed the crowd up the hill, and I stood in the back and watched Him die. I was not a religious person, but on that day, when I saw what the soldiers did to Him and heard what He said as He hung limply on the cross, I could feel something change deep within me.

"I heard Him say, 'Father, forgive them, for they know not what they do' [Luke 23:34, KJV]. He was in deep agony and suffered terribly. At the moment of His death, the sky darkened, and the Earth shook beneath my feet. The ground actually moved. The next day, I was tormented with guilt. Why was I set free, and why did He have to die? Some people told me He was an innocent man, a Teacher

47. Matthew 27:17.

and a Rabbi who only went about doing good, healing people of their diseases, and teaching them about the love of God.[48]

"For a few days following His death, I went to that hill and just sat there. I looked up at the overcast sky and thought about God—someone I had not thought about before. I began to talk to Him, and I asked Him if He could forgive me. Then, suddenly, as I sat there, I felt an overwhelming sense of peace. I knew, then, that my prayer was answered. God forgave me. I just knew it. That was the first time I had ever prayed.

"I know you men came from Rome seeking answers about what happened here, including His resurrection three days later. I didn't see His resurrected body as some have said they did. But I can tell you that during my lifetime, I have met many people, and I've had many experiences, but nothing can compare to what happened on the hill the day He died. Jesus was no ordinary person, and because of what I experienced, I am a completely different man. My whole outlook has changed. I no longer see men

48. Luke 23:34, 44–45; Matthew 27:51.

as opportunities to use or take advantage of. I no longer walk around just waiting for a reason to punch someone in the face.

"No, seeing Jesus on the cross took the anger from my heart and the sword from my hand. Instead, all I want to do now is to tell everyone I meet about Him and what happened to me. That's my story." Barabbas paused, then continued, "As I listen to myself speak, I am amazed at my own words. I am someone who lived their whole life and never even thought about God, who He is, what He is like. To be very honest, He was completely irrelevant to me. But everything has changed since that day I saw Him die. I see things so differently now."

One of the senators asked Barabbas, "Why do you think the crowd chose you instead of Jesus?"

"I don't know. I've thought about that often. Someone told me that it was all prearranged by the Jewish authorities. They planted people in the crowd to shout very loud. Even though I didn't have anything to do with that, I felt guilty."

Another senator asked him, "Why do you think the

Jews hated Jesus, especially since He was a Rabbi, and it is reported that He went around only doing good?"

Barabbas replied, "I talked to some Jews about that. I think the main reason was because He claimed to be equal with God. That was considered to be blasphemy in the eyes of the religious Jews. I can understand that. They worshipped a holy God, and they saw Jesus as only a man.[49]

"You'll never believe this, but I've been reading the Bible, and I think the Jewish leaders forgot that the God who created all there is out of nothing could easily have decided to appear in a human body. The Scriptures say that with Him, all things are possible. Just look at me. Who would have thought that, one day, I would be quoting from the Bible! Another reason I think the Jewish leaders hated Jesus," Barabbas continued, "was because the miracles He performed and the large group who followed Him posed a threat to their power and influence. Also, He was very critical of them."[50]

"Why?" interjected one of the senators.

---

49. Matt 26:65.
50. John 11:45-48.

"I'm told because He thought they were focused on very small things and overlooked the more important things. That's really all I can tell you because that is all I know."[51]

The three senators thanked Barabbas, and he was ushered out the door.

The next and final witness was a nicely dressed woman. She sat in the chair and said, "Hello, my name is Mary. I was born in Magdala, near the coastline of the Sea of Galilee. One day, this man called Jesus visited our town. He was a Teacher, a Rabbi, and Healer. He healed many, including me. I was considered an outcast in my town because I was possessed by demons."

One senator interrupted her, "What are demons?"

"They are bad spirits," she answered. "I didn't know they were living in me until I met this man called Jesus. I always knew I was very troubled and not like other people. My erratic behavior scared people, and they fled from me. I had no control over the dark forces I felt inside me. They were powerful. I said and did things that I didn't understand.

51. Matthew 23:33; Luke 11:42.

Sometimes, I felt like I was a puppet, and someone else was pulling the strings. It was awful. There was nowhere I could go for help. Then, one day, Jesus came to Magdala. He was teaching and healing people in the crowd. I approached Him, and His eyes caught mine. He looked at me intensely and reached out and touched me on my head. He said, 'Woman, be healed.' Suddenly, I felt something unusual in my whole body. I felt light and free for the first time in my life. It was as if I was unshackled. I looked around me, and everything looked different. I looked up into His face, and He smiled and said, 'Follow Me, Mary.' I don't know why, but everywhere He went with His disciples, I went too. And they didn't seem to mind.[52]

"When the terrible end came, and He was carrying that heavy cross up the hill, I slowly walked with the crowd who followed behind Him. Mary, His mother, was with me. My heart was very heavy, and I couldn't stop crying. I just couldn't look at His mother. We held on to each other for support. I don't understand why He had to die at such a young age and experience such a cruel death.

52. Luke 8:2.

I had seen someone crucified before, and I knew what agony awaited Him.

"Once, He explained to the disciples and me that He had come into the world to bring a message from His Father, and that once His work was done, He would be returning to the place He had come from. He said that the message He was bringing had to be sealed with His blood and that was why He had to die. I don't think any of us really understood what He was saying.

"At those times when He, the disciples, and I sat around the campfire in the desert, I would look at Him and think to myself, *Surely, this man came from somewhere else.* Even the things He taught us sounded different from anything we had heard before.

"He told us, 'Blessed are the poor in spirit [the humble] for theirs is the kingdom of heaven. Blessed are those who mourn for they will be comforted… Blessed are those who are persecuted because of righteousness, for theirs is the kingdom of heaven' [Matthew 5:3–4, 10, NIV].

"He even told us to love our enemies, and that in

His kingdom, the last would be first. The disciples and I listened to Him, not saying a word. We were mesmerized not only by what He was saying but by Him. He spoke with great authority.

"After Jesus was sentenced to die, His mother, Mary, and I followed Jesus up the hill. He was carrying the heavy cross. I would have given my life for His if I could have. He was so kind and loving and had helped and healed so many people—the blind, the lame, and people like me. Many of them were in the crowd following Him up that hill. The only sounds which could be heard were the women weeping and the shuffle of our sandals on the ground.

"We followed Him all the way to the top of the hill and watched the soldiers nail Him and two other men to the crosses. As the crosses were lifted up and placed securely in the ground, we turned our heads away. We could hear their groans and cries of pain. It was horrible. Mary and I clung to each other. We were both crying uncontrollably. We stayed with Him the whole time, and at the very end, we could hear Him say, 'Father forgive them, for they know not what they do.' [Luke 23:34, ESV]. Then, He took one more deep breath, bowed His head, and died. At that moment, the sky turned very dark, the Earth shook beneath our feet. It was over. I saw a soldier approach Him with a spear and plunge it into His side. Blood and water spilled out. I don't know why he had to do that. It was obvious He was dead. Two prominent Jewish men took His body down from the cross and carried it away to a nearby tomb.

"After a while, all of us who had remained to the bitter end walked down the hill. No one said a word. We all returned to our homes. Later, I remembered that He had told us that after three days, He would rise again. After seeing Him die such a horrible death, I really couldn't imagine how something like that could happen to Jesus. He had helped so many people and even performed miracles. It just didn't make sense to me. When I reached my home, I was so exhausted that I fell into bed and slept through to the next morning—a Saturday. That day, I thought a lot about the events of Friday and about what He had said about rising from the dead. I had seen Him raise Lazarus from the dead, so I began to consider it a possibility. I thought if anyone could do it, He could. I spent the day with my family and friends and went to sleep early.

"The next day was Sunday. I awoke earlier than usual. The sunlight was streaming through my window. I heard a knock at my door. Two women from the town were standing there. They reminded me that we had said we would go to the tomb to properly prepare His body. I dressed quickly, and we hurried to the place where they had put Him. The morning sun was breaking in the sky. When we arrived, we saw that the heavy stone was rolled away. My heart began to race with excitement! Could it be? Could He be alive?

"I looked inside the tomb. Jesus wasn't there. Instead, I saw two men dressed in white. They told us that Jesus was not there and that we should go tell His disciples that He had risen from the dead just as He said He would.

"The other two women returned to town and told everyone, but I stayed behind. I couldn't believe it. I sat down on one of the huge garden rocks to rest a while.

Then, I saw a man walking in the garden. I thought He was the gardener, so I approached Him.

"I was a little frantic and breathless and asked Him if he knew what happened to the man who was in the tomb. He turned completely around, looked at me, and said, '*Mary.*' I was shocked. It was Jesus. I hadn't recognized Him because His appearance had changed, but I recognized His voice when He said my name. I cried out, 'Rabboni,' and tried to reach out and touch Him. But He took a step back and said, 'Don't touch Me yet, I haven't ascended to my Father.'[53] I began to cry again, but this time, it was tears of joy. I returned to the town. The news had traveled quickly. Everyone was talking about Jesus and the empty tomb."

The three senators at the long rectangular table were leaning over, listening intently to what Mary was telling them.

She continued, "I know that the three of you are Roman senators and were sent from Rome to find out what happened here. I have told you my story, but there are many more. I have a feeling that this is just the beginning."

53. John 20:17.

Mary's eyes filled with tears.

One of the senators asked her, "What do you mean that this is just the beginning?"

Mary replied, "I can't explain it. I just have a feeling that, one day, His story and teachings will be heard far beyond Judea and Rome."

Another senator said, "That's a little farfetched don't you think? You said yourself that you saw Him die. Maybe, it really was the gardener you saw at the tomb."

Mary replied, "No. He's alive! I saw Him, and I spoke to Him. He has risen, just as He said He would."

The senators rose to their feet and thanked Mary for sharing her story with them and escorted her to the door. They walked over to another part of the room where there were jars of wine and three glasses on a small table. They filled their glasses and began to talk among themselves. One of them said, "I never heard anything like these stories, but I think they are just that—'stories.' Some were probably exaggerated. I think it is safe to say that we can take back a report to Rome and tell them that there is nothing to fear.

In a few months, no one will remember what happened here in Judea." The other two senators agreed.

The lights on stage began to dim, and the curtain slowly descended. The lights in the theatre came on.

The pastor of the church next door to the theatre annex appeared on stage and said, "Thank you for coming today. All of the witnesses you saw represented real people whose lives were changed when they met Jesus. We took dramatic license and added a little to their stories, but essentially, what they shared was true. I know in an audience of this size, there are followers of Jesus, those who may be considering following Him, those from other faiths, and some who don't believe in God at all. Everyone is welcome here. We believe Jesus is alive today and is knocking at your door. He wants to enter into your heart and change your live forever. Don't let this opportunity pass you by. You are not here by accident but by divine appointment. If you would like to speak to me or any of our staff, we will be available in the front of the auditorium. Thank you again for coming, and God bless you."

CHAPTER 8

Becky turned to Barbara saying, "Do you want to speak to someone? I don't. I want to be quiet and digest all that we saw. I think Mary was right, it was just the beginning. And did you notice, she called Jesus 'Rabboni.' I came across the word yesterday and looked it up. It means Rabbi in Aramaic—the language which was spoken at that time. It seems a lot of people called Jesus "Rabbi." I wonder how all of that changed. I'm going to ask Him the next time we talk."

Barbara said, "Well, just think, you can actually talk to Him and ask Him questions."

Becky and Barbara left the theatre and walked toward home. Becky said, "I think I want to help spread Jesus's message. People need to know. I will ask Him what I should do and where I should go." Becky and Barbara walked for a little while, then said goodbye.

Becky, preoccupied by her thoughts, walked slowly to her house. Deeply affected by the play she had just seen, she climbed the steps and opened the front door. As she entered the house, she could tell that her mother had been cooking. There was no mistaking the aroma of her favorite meal—pot roast. No one could cook pot roast like her mother. Becky saw that her father and her brother, Charlie, were playing Scrabble in the dining room.

Her mother greeted her and asked her how she spent the day. "I will tell you later," Becky replied. "I'm going upstairs for a while. I'm tired." As she climbed the stairs to her bedroom, she hoped that Jesus would pay her another visit. She was beginning to look forward to His visits.

This was her favorite time of day. With the sun just beginning to set, she opened the window and looked up at the sky outside her room and thought, *God is an artist.* She wondered how anyone could look at the sky, especially at sunrise and sunset, and not think about God's creativity. The colors at those particular times are absolutely breathtaking. *What an amazing palette He must hold in His hand,* she thought.

She adjusted the blinds in her room, so the soft golden glow of the setting sun filled her room. She sat in her rocking chair, thinking of the play she just saw and the witnesses who told their stories. *Some of the witnesses took me back in time,* she thought. *After hearing all of these stories, I don't know how anyone could not believe that Jesus was the Messiah. How did they miss it? How could people today think that He didn't exist with so much evidence to the contrary?"* As she thought about the day's events, she saw the colorful circle begin to take shape in front of her. As usual, Jesus appeared in the center of the swirl of many colors. He smiled and asked Becky how she enjoyed the play.

She said, "I really liked it. I learned so much."

"What did you learn?" He asked her.

"Well," Becky replied, "I learned that You impacted the lives of many people. I especially liked Gamaliel's story. He was very honest, admitting that maybe a terrible mistake was made. I think so too.[54] I don't understand how the Jewish people made such a mistake, and I don't understand how You became 'the other God,' as my grandmother says. I think that's probably how most Jews see You. How did that happen? How did You become 'the other God' when You are the Messiah of Israel and the God of Israel?"[55]

Jesus paused and replied, "Becky, most of the people who believed in Me in the beginning were Jewish. Some were Gentiles. However, not everyone believed, and there were many arguments about Me between those who believed and those who did not. Those Jews who believed that I was the Messiah called themselves Jewish Christians—followers of Me, the Christ or the Anointed One. Those Jews who did not believe retained their Jewish identity as it always was. The Gentiles who believed were

---

54. Acts 5:34–39.
55. Romans 11:25.

called Christians. It is the same today. And that is how it has been down through the centuries. However, from a long-term perspective, I came to break down the wall that divides the Jew and the Gentile."[56]

Becky was confused. "So if I believe in You and want to follow You, what do I call myself? Am I a Jewish believer, a Christian, or a Jewish Christian? I don't want to give up being Jewish. It's very important to me."

Jesus said, "I'll explain it this way. It was the God of Israel—the God of Abraham, Isaac, and Jacob—who sent Me into the world as the Messiah. Savior. Redeemer. I am His Son. The concept of a Messiah is rooted in Judaism. By accepting and acknowledging Me as your Messiah, you are being completely obedient to God and following the path We laid out. It is the only path to obtain forgiveness, salvation, and a restored relationship with Us. The Godhead has three aspects—Father, Son, and Holy Spirit. I am God's only Son. When I came to Earth, I took on a human form, just like Barabbas described in the play. However, I never relinquished My divinity and My relationship with My

56. Acts 11:19; Ephesians 2:14.

Father and the Holy Spirit. When I was with My disciples I told them, 'Whoever has seen Me, has seen My Father' [John 14:9, ESV]. By accepting Me as your Messiah, you are making God and Our Word—the Holy Scriptures—the centerpiece and heartbeat of your faith.[57]

"It is not the traditions of men and the outward ceremonies that are important. I look at a man's heart. That's why the religious leaders in My day did not recognize Me. They were focused on the externals and the outer rituals, not the inner life and the heart.[58]

"If you accept Me as your Savior, you are still a Jew. You become a Jew who has accepted the long-promised Messiah of Israel in fulfillment of My Word. That makes you a true believer because you are one inwardly. The redemptive plan was offered first to the Jew and then to the Gentile. It's now a message that the whole world needs to hear. Becky, you are not turning your back on the Jewish people. If you accept Me, you become more of a Jew than you have ever been because you are being completely obedient to the

---

57. John 1:1, 14, 14:9.
58. 1 Samuel 16:17; Matthew 9:13.

God of Israel. Always remember, the important thing is what God thinks, not what people think, no matter how influential they are."[59]

Becky protested, "But people say, 'Jews don't believe in Jesus.' They say that as if it were part of their identity as a Jew."

"I know," Jesus replied, "but I believe they are strong and mature enough to hear the whole truth, recognize their mistake of rejecting Me, acknowledge it, and someday, return to Me as My people. That is why I am still reaching out to them. When you love someone, you don't write them off. Today, some Jews are returning to Me. One day, a very large number of the Jewish people will believe in Me. So it is written."[60]

"I have a question for You. When I was in Hebrew school, I remember reading the Shema. It says, 'Hear, O Israel: the Lord our God, the Lord is one'" (Deuteronomy 6:4, NIV). Then, Becky smiled, "But You probably know what it says.

---

59. Romans 2:23–29.
60. Zechariah 12:8–10, 14:3.

"You mentioned Your Father several times. And Christians call You His Son, and then, there is the Holy Spirit. That much I understand. My question is, how then can God be one and three at the same time?"

Jesus answered, "Moses wrote his portion of the Scriptures under the guidance of the Holy Spirit [the Ruach HaKodesh]. When he wrote 'one,' he chose the word 'echad.' It indicates oneness as a cluster of grapes is one. He could have chosen another word and that is 'yachid' to signify absolute oneness, as a single grape is one. It is interesting to note that when My Father and I were instituting the holy state of matrimony [Genesis 2:24], we instructed the husband and wife to become 'one flesh.' Here again, the word 'echad' is used.[61]

"There are other references to the plurality of the Godhead in the Older Testament. In Genesis 11, when the Tower of Babel was being built, and it displeased Us, We said, 'Come, let *Us* go down and confuse [mix up] their language so they will not understand each other'" (Genesis 11:7, NIV).

61. Compare/contrast Deuteronomy 6:4 (BHS) and Gen 22:2, 12 (BHS).

"We never discussed this in my Hebrew class," said Becky. "I did hear about the Ruach HaKodesh. So is that the same Holy Spirit that is in the Newer Testament?"

"Yes, there is only one Holy Spirit. The Holy Spirit that hovered over the face of the waters during creation in the first book of the Torah [Genesis 1:2] is the same Holy Spirit who descended upon Me in the form of a dove at My baptism when all who were there heard My Father say, 'This is My beloved Son, with whom I am well pleased' [Matthew 3:17, ESV]. The Trinity can be clearly seen here. My Father who is in heaven is speaking. I am being baptized in water on the Earth, and the Holy Spirit descends upon Me in the form of a dove."

"Wow, that's amazing! I've been reading my Bible a lot these past few days. After meeting and talking to You and seeing the play, 'The Tribunal,' I am now convinced that You are the promised Messiah of Israel. As You know, accepting You as my Savior will cause a great upheaval in my home. Everyone is already very upset at the mere mention of Your name. However, I want to do the right thing. Before I take the next step, would it be all right if I ask You a few more questions? Do You have time?"

He smiled. "Of course, I have time."

"Every year, on Yom Kippur, my family and I fast all day, and we spend most of the day in temple. The rabbi told us this is the day we atone for our sins of the previous year. He told us that it is the day we have an opportunity to make things right with God and other people. My family and I are always very careful to follow all of the instructions. I always thought this was enough. Now, after reading the Newer Testament, I am beginning to see that this may not be true. Have we been doing it the wrong way?"

"No, Becky, you and your family followed the instructions as far as they went in the Older Testament, but those Scriptures don't reveal the whole truth. The ceremonies in the Older Testament were only a type or foreshadowing of what was to come later.[62]

"Yom Kippur is derived from the Hebrew word 'kaphar,' which means to "cover over." In other words, at that time, the sins of Our people—the Jews—were

62. Hebrew 8:5; 10:1.

covered. They were not meant to be totally removed until the Messiah would come. Do you remember reading in the Newer Testament that when John the Baptist saw Me, he said, 'Behold the lamb of God who *takes away* the sins of the world' [John 1:29, ESV]. According to My timetable, when I entered Earth, the time had come for the sins of the world to be completely removed. They would no longer just be covered. Once the sins were removed, sinful men and women could then approach a Holy God. The unassailable barrier which existed between man and God was now torn down. And it was I who did it. I am the only one who could do it.[63]

"Now that you are reading the Scriptures, Becky, do you remember reading that at the exact moment I died on the cross, there were earthquakes? The ground shook violently, and the curtain in the temple was torn in two. Up until that time, there was a curtain in the temple which separated the outer chamber, called the holy room, and the inner chamber, called the holy of holies. Only the high priest could enter the holy of

---

63. Psalms 3:1, 85:2 and John 1:29.

holies and only on one day a year—Yom Kippur, the Day of Atonement. He entered to make atonement for himself and for the sins of Our people.[64]

"The curtain symbolized the barrier between man and God. On the curtain, itself, were beautiful representations of cherubim woven into the tapestry. They were pictures of the same cherubim which stood guard at the entrance to the Garden of Eden after the fall. They prevented Adam and Eve from reentering the garden. They also barred the way into My presence.[65]

"At the exact moment I died on the cross, the sky grew dark, and there was a strong earthquake, and the thick curtain was torn in two from top to bottom, signifying that the hand of God tore it, and now, it was possible to approach Us. My Father and I made a way where, before, there was no way. That's Our signature, Becky."

"What is?" Becky asked.

"Making a way where there is no way!" Jesus replied.

Becky asked, "Why are You called, 'Jesus, the Christ.'

---

64. Luke 23:44–45.
65. Genesis 3:24.

What does that mean?"

"The original meaning comes from the Greek word *Christos* which means 'Anointed One.' That's what Messiah means. *Christos* was the Greek term that Bible translators used for the Hebrew word *Mashiach*."

"Sometimes, You are called 'The Redeemer' and a 'ransom' is mentioned. What does that mean?" asked Becky.

"I will answer your question by telling you this little story written by one of My followers. Once, there was a young boy who carved a boat out of wood. He loved that boat and often took it to the nearby ocean and watched it bob along and drift back-and-forth with the tide. One day, a sudden storm arose, and a gust of wind took it far from the shore. It was out of his reach, and because of the teeming rain, he had to quickly return home. Many months passed. The boy missed his boat very much. Then, one day, he was walking in his village, and he passed the toy shop. To his surprise, he saw his boat in the window. He rushed into the store and told the owner that the boat belonged to him. However, the owner argued with the boy and refused to give him the boat. So the boy offered to buy the boat, and the owner agreed to sell it to him. The boy left the store, holding his beloved boat close to his heart. If someone were close enough to hear him, they could hear him talking to the boat saying, 'Now, you are twice mine. Once because I made you, and now, twice because I bought you.'[66]

"That's really the meaning of redemption. My Father and I created mankind, but because of the fall, we were separated. It felt like I had lost them because they were once Mine. That's why I came into the world—to seek and save them. The price I paid for their salvation was My blood. In My heart, I feel very much like that little boy. All who accept Me as their Savior are twice Mine. Once because I made them, and twice because I saved or redeemed them. Like that boy and his boat, I hold My followers close to My heart. They are My children."[67]

Becky said, "That's a beautiful story, but there is

66. Gurley, *Twice Yours.*
67. Several Greek words are used to capture the broad concept of redemption in the NT—agorazō, "to buy or ransom," lytroō, "to redeem," and exagorazō, "to take out of the marketplace."

something I don't understand. Why didn't the Jewish leaders recognize you as their Messiah?"

"There were many reasons, Becky. Some of them, including a few of My disciples as well, were looking for a Messiah who would be a political leader and deliver them from the oppression of Rome. They didn't know that I had come to deliver them from the greater oppression of sin and sin's penalty which is death.[68]

"But the main reason was that the majority of the religious leaders were trying to achieve righteousness in My sight by keeping the Law of Moses. The law was never intended to give man a righteous standing with God. It was only meant to reveal man's sinfulness and to point him to the only One who could make him righteous and that was Me. A man's works will never make him righteous or worthy in My eyes. It is something that only I can do."[69]

"I have another question," said Becky. "Actually, this one is from my friend, Barbara. What does it mean to be 'born again?'"

---

68. John 8:31–35.
69. Rom 8:2–3.

"Because of the fall and the resulting consequences, people are born spiritually dead [no spiritual life and separated from Me]. Until they realize this, they won't recognize they need a Savior—someone who will deliver them from the darkness which envelops them. The sad state in which all of mankind lives is that they don't know their true standing before God. They can't see God clearly, and they can't see themselves clearly. They are spiritually blind, and part of the blindness is not knowing this is true.[70]

"Satan's plan is to keep them in the dark. But God overruled Satan's plan and sent Me to bring man out of the darkness of sin and into the light. In the same way that you see things clearly when you turn on the light in a dark room, in the light of My presence, you can see Me and yourself more clearly. One of the things men will see is that I am holy, and they are sinful, in need of forgiveness and redemption.[71]

"Your first birth gives you physical life. The second birth [when you accept Me as your Savior] gives you

---

70. John 3:3-16.
71. 2 Cor 11:14; John 3:19–21.

spiritual life. That's the meaning of the term 'born again.' Man's first birth ends in eternal separation from Me in a place of torment forever. That is the legacy of Adam's disobedience. All of mankind inherits that legacy when he or she is born. It is the judgment of God on sin. It doesn't matter how good or bad you are. Your destiny is set like railroad tracks.[72]

"All of your good works or bad works won't change the position of the tracks. The train travels the way the tracks are set. It can do nothing else. However, when a person has an encounter with Me and accepts Me as Savior, I change the direction of the tracks much like the railroad switchman does. Now, the train has a new direction and destination. And further, I am now on board the train. The new destination is life eternal with Me in heaven. There is a lot more that happens when you accept Me as your Savior, but for now, I think this simple explanation will help you make your final decision about Me."[73]

"I am beginning to see the picture, but that brings up

---

72. John 3:3–16.
73. John 3:36; 5:24.

another question. May I speak frankly?"

"Of course."

"What You've described doesn't sound inclusive. Actually, it sounds exclusive. Only certain people are on the train that is going to heaven. There is only one train track that leads to heaven. Is that correct?"

"Yes," Jesus said. "There is only one way to enter the kingdom of God and that is through Me."[74]

"Please don't be mad at me for saying this, but I don't think that is very loving. What about the other people? You said You created everyone."[75]

"I'm not upset that you asked that question, Becky." Jesus's voice was kind and patient. "People have always been upset that I taught that there is only one way. Instead of being grateful that there is a way, they focus instead on the fact that there is only one way. They forget that I suffered and died to create that way!"[76]

"Do all the other people go to hell? Is there really such a place?"

74. John 14:6.
75. John 3:19–20.
76. John 3:16.

"Yes, Becky, there is such a place, but no one need go there if they follow Me."[77]

"I have one more question. I'm sorry I have so many questions, but I need to understand what it is you are teaching, and it is very difficult. Your teaching is very different from what I have heard in my home, in Hebrew school, in high school, and now college. Actually, the world doesn't think like You do."

"You are right, Becky, it doesn't. Take your time. Ask your question."

"Are you saying that only the people who accept You as Savior are considered 'children of God?' If You and Your Father created everyone and love everyone, don't You consider all of them Your children?"

"Unfortunately, no. While it is true that I created everyone, not everyone will believe and follow Me. In order to become My child, a new birth is necessary and that can only happen through Me and the work that I did on the cross. When you are born the first time, you are spiritually disconnected from Me. It is only the second birth that

77. John 3:36; 5:24.

connects you to Me and enables you to become part of My family, 'the family of God.' You need spiritual life to connect to Me because I am Spirit. The first birth doesn't give this to you. It keeps you earthbound, destined for hell. Only the second birth gives you spiritual life, connects you to Me, sets you free, en route to heaven."[78]

"My friend, Barbara, and I once talked about heaven and hell. Do You know what her guru told her? He told her that everyone is born divine, and we just have to discover the divinity within ourselves, and we can be like God. He said that a poet once described it as 'the imprisoned splendor' which resides within."[79]

Jesus looked intently into Becky's eyes. "Now, Becky, I am going to give you your first quiz. Who does that remind you of?"

She thought for a moment and replied, "It reminds me of Satan. He wants to be like God. So Barbara's teacher is not teaching her the truth, is he?"

78. John 1:12; 3:3.
79. Browning, Robert. *Paracelsus.* Part I Paracelsus Aspires,

https://ebooks.adelaide.edu.au/b/browning/robert/paracelsus/index.html (March 27, 2016).

"No, he's not. He's putting forth a lie—a lie he believes himself. Man is not born divine. He is born a sinner. Let's look at the reason for the lie, Becky. If man is born divine, does he need a Savior?" Jesus asked.[80]

"Now that You put it that way, no, he doesn't."

"Lies are one of Satan's strategies to keep mankind away from the truth that will set him free and away from the cross which will ultimately save him," Jesus said.[81]

"One last question, please. I promise."

Jesus smiled and shook His head yes.

"What does it mean to be saved by grace? I heard that expression recently."

"Man, in his sinful state, does not have a righteousness of his own. He may do good works and live a moral life, but his intrinsic nature is sinful. When someone accepts Me as their Savior, they are covered with My righteousness and that is how My Father sees them—clothed in My robe of righteousness. In other words, when He looks upon a follower of Mine, He sees Me. My righteousness covers all

---

80. John 8:44; Psalms 51:5.
81. 2 Corinthians 11:14–15.

of the believer's sins. The Psalmist David wrote '…as far as the east is from the west, so far has He removed our transgressions from us' [Psalm 103:12, NIV]. Why is this grace? Because it is a gift. Mankind does not deserve it, cannot earn it, and will never be worthy of it."[82]

"When you describe it that way, I can't help but wonder why people reject such a magnificent gift. It doesn't make sense. I guess they just don't understand. But I'm beginning to. Thank You so much for being patient and answering all of my questions," she said. "I feel, in my heart, I am now ready to accept You as my Messiah. How do I do that? I know that it is going to create havoc in my family."

"I'm so happy, Becky, and all of the witnesses in heaven are clapping their hands![83] I can hear them. As we begin, please examine your heart and make sure that what you are saying comes from your heart."

Becky got down on her knees before Jesus, and He guided her with these words: "Jesus, I recognize that I am

---

82. Ephesians 2:8–9.
83. Luke 15:10.

a sinner and that You are a Holy God, the only true and living God. I acknowledge that I am in need of a Savior and that You died on the cross to save me and pay the debt for all my sins. Thank You for paying a debt I couldn't pay. It is paid in full. Please forgive me for all of my offenses in Your sight and set me free from the bondage of sin.[84] Create in me a clean heart in which You can come to dwell and fill me with Your Holy Spirit.

Give me a new life in You, and someday, may You be glorified in my life. Amen."

Becky repeated this prayer and eagerly looked up to Jesus for approval.

"Becky, you now belong to Me," He said. "You are Mine now and for all eternity. I am so pleased."[85]

Becky breathed a sigh of relief and rose to her feet. "I have been struggling with this for a while. I felt we were moving toward this moment. Now that it is done, what do I do next?"

Jesus told her, "I will reveal it to you one step at a

---

84. Colossians 2:13–14.
85. Romans 8:37–39.

time.[86] Now, it is time to go and tell your parents. They need to know. However, be kind and gentle with them. They will not understand. Remember, be strong and courageous. I am with you." With these words, Jesus disappeared in the swirl of many colors.

Becky took a deep breath, saying out loud, "Well, here goes nothing!" She went downstairs to the kitchen. Her mother had just put the pot roast on the table. After dinner, she said to her parents and Charlie, "I have something to tell you." She hesitated a bit and then said, "After much study and prayer, I have come to the conclusion that Jesus is the Messiah of Israel, and I want to become one of His followers."

Her mother gasped in shock. "You can't be serious!"

Her father shook his head. "I knew this was going to happen. I saw it coming." Charlie almost choked on his dessert and said, "Here we go!"

"I know that this is going to be very difficult for all of you, especially Grandma, but I'm grown up now. I'm eighteen and can make my own choices. This is very

86. 2 Corinthians 5:7.

important to me," Becky said.

"Becky," her mother said, "we've tried to be good parents. You know we did everything we could to provide a good life for you. How could you disgrace our family like this?"

"I'm not disgracing anyone. There is a lot of confusion about who Jesus really is. That's not my fault. You know that since I was a little girl, I've wanted to know God. I'm sorry that it turns out to be Jesus. No, let me take that back. I'm not sorry it is Jesus."

Her father appealed to their standing in the community. "Becky, have you thought about the consequences? What will our family and friends think? What will our Jewish neighbors think? We live in a Jewish community."

"I'm sorry, but I can't live my life depending upon what others think. If I do, I'll be like a yo-yo. Up one day, down the next. People's opinions change with the prevailing wind. There is only one person whose opinion matters to me and that is God's. And it just happens to be Jesus. Mom and Dad, I don't want to cause you pain and unhappiness. I love you both very much. I didn't plan this. It just happened."

Becky's mother was crying now. "How did we fail you? We must have done something wrong."

Tears came down Becky's cheeks as well. "No, you and Dad haven't failed me. You just don't understand. You know me well. I wouldn't hurt either of you or Grandma for the world. I have been reading the Older and Newer Testaments, and it turns out that Jesus is the promised Messiah—the Mashiach. He loves the Jewish people very much and wants to be reunited with us. Not only was He Jewish, but He was a Rabbi. Did you know He was a Rabbi? I didn't."

Becky's father said, "He told you this? You've been talking to Him? Becky, I know your breakup with Louis a few months ago was a huge disappointment but escaping into fantasy is not helpful. Neither is taking drugs. I know that a lot of young people experiment with drugs. They think it's cool. If that's the case, your mother and I will help you. But if you choose to follow

Jesus, we can't help you. You do it alone. We are Jewish, and we will never be Christians. Never!"

Becky drew in her breath. "Well, I really didn't expect anything different than this. I have one more thing to tell you. I've been reevaluating everything. I am thinking of finishing my college education in the Hebrew University in Jerusalem."

"What? Why are you going to do that?" her father said.

"I want to get familiar with the country and the people. I am beginning to believe God wants me to be a missionary to the Jewish people, and I think He wants me to go to Israel."

Becky's mother gasped, saying, "Now, I know that you have completely lost your mind!"

"Tell me," said her father, "how are you going to pay for this?"

"You know I have a bank account. Over the years, I've saved all my money from my birthday gifts, my Bat Mitzvah, and my sweet sixteen party. It may not be enough for the whole three years, but it will give me a good start, and I can get a part-time job."

Becky's father was really angry now. "I will close out the account today. My name is also on the account, and the bank manager is a friend of mine."

"I anticipated that, so I drew out most of the money yesterday. You know, Dad, I am no longer a child. I am almost an adult now." Becky raised her voice and said. "It is my life!"

Becky's father yelled, "This discussion is over." He got up from the table and left the room saying, "I can't believe this is happening."

Becky tried unsuccessfully to comfort her mother. She returned to her room and picked up her new Bible and began to read the Psalms to comfort herself. She turned to Psalm 91 and read, "He who dwells in the shelter of the Most High will abide in the shadow of the Almighty. I will say to the Lord, My refuge and my fortress, my God, in whom I trust" (Psalm 91:1–2, ESV).

She said to herself, "That's what I will do. I will hide myself in the shelter of His wings. There, I will be safe."

She turned off the lamp near her bed and lay down. Tears filled her eyes, and she said out loud. "This is so hard. Why wasn't I born into a Christian family?" Then, she drifted off to sleep.

CHAPTER 9

In the morning, she awoke a little later than usual. She dressed and went downstairs. Her parents and Charlie were not around, but to her surprise, her grandmother was seated at the breakfast table. She said to Becky, "Your parents and Charlie went out for a while. They are very upset about your so-called conversion and your plans to be a Christian missionary.

"Becky, you know that I love you, but you are making the biggest mistake of your life. Let me tell you something about my early life which I don't think you know. I was born in Austria in 1930. The world stage was being set for World War II. It really wasn't safe to be a Jew at that time. Anti-Semitism was prevalent and growing. My father owned a store in a small Austrian town, and he and my mother worked very hard to earn a living. We lived a simple life and tried to avoid any kind of trouble. One night, November 9, 1938, to be exact, a truckload of German soldiers, carrying rifles, suddenly appeared and filled the streets of our town.

"They smashed Jewish-owned stores, including my father's. Many buildings and synagogues were also destroyed. Some were set on fire. This hate-filled rampage occurred throughout Germany and Austria. That night became known around the whole world as 'Kristallnacht, Night of the Broken Glass' because of the broken glass which littered the streets.

"A lot of Jewish people died that night. Others were severely beaten. Many were arrested. My family was fortunate. My father had anticipated something like that, and our bags were already packed. My parents, my brother, sister, and I escaped. Each of us carried one bag of belongings. We left everything else behind. Because we were in such a hurry, we forgot to take some food we had prepared.

"I remember my mother crying and saying to us, 'Children, we have to be very brave. We have to leave our home and find somewhere else to live.' I began to cry too, and I asked my mother, 'Why do we have to leave?' And she said, 'It is not safe here. We are Jewish.'

"As we traveled under cover of the night, I remember it was cold and damp, and we were very hungry. On the way, we met another Jewish family who were also fleeing. All of us found a small clearing in the woods and sat down to rest a while. The other family had some food which they shared with us. As we were eating, I happened to look at my father, and he was quietly crying. That was the first time I had ever seen my father cry.

"We finally snuck across the border into Hungary, one by one. In the distance, we could hear the Nazi guard dogs barking. It pierced the silence of the night and filled our hearts with fear. We found temporary shelter on a farm, and shortly thereafter, we were able to come to America. My mother had relatives here, and they helped us get passage on a ship. With God's help, we were able to start a new life here in Brooklyn, but I will never forget 'Kristallnacht!'

"I can still hear the sounds of the soldiers smashing the store windows, the screams of people being beaten and killed, and the cries of men and women reaching out to their loved ones as they helplessly watched them being tossed into trucks like sacks of potatoes. But it is the sound of crying babies that I will always remember. It was as if they instinctively knew that something terrible was taking place. Overnight, many of them became orphans because of the carnage that took place.

"Do you know what else I remember? I remember the crosses on the uniforms of the soldiers. It was a hooked cross, and it became the symbol of the emerging Nazi killing machine. You may not know this, but the swastika, as it is called, found its way into some churches because the lines between the political agenda of Germany and the spiritual message of the church became blurred for a period of time.[87]

"To me and so many other Jews, the image of the cross became a symbol of death. It will always mean that to me. There's so much you don't know about that era, Becky. It is so important to be informed before making such a life-changing decision.

"I read somewhere that Hitler first saw that cross—the swastika—in a church when he was a young boy. It was carved into one of the walls. Later, when he grew up, he remembered it, and he used it as a centerpiece of the Nazi party's flag. When he was a young man, he was an aspiring artist. In 1920, he designed the flag for the Nationalist Socialist Party. When he became chancellor of Germany in 1933, he ordered that one of the national flags of Germany would be the swastika flag. It soon became a symbol of anti-Semitism around the world and continues to be so to this day. Becky, I never thought I'd

87. There were many Christians in Germany who bravely resisted the Nazis and paid for it with their lives. One such Christian was a very courageous Protestant pastor, Dietrich Bonhoeffer. He was executed by the Nazis in April 1945, shortly before the end of WWII.

live to see the day when my daughter's daughter would turn her back on the Jewish people to follow, as you call it, 'Jesus and the way of the cross.'"

By this time, Becky was crying. She took her grandmother in her arms and said, "I'm so sorry you had to go through all of that, but none of what you described has anything to do with Jesus. He was a Jew too. And He was very familiar with suffering. He's the promised Messiah of Israel, and He didn't come to kill or hurt the Jewish people. He came to give us life. New life. And Grandma, I haven't turned my back on the Jewish people. I am still a Jew and will always be a Jew." Becky's voice was rising, "I will never, ever give that up! It is part of who I am, and it is deeply ingrained in my heart. No one, not even you, Grandma, can tell me that I am no longer Jewish because I have accepted Jesus as my Messiah.

"For some reason, many Jewish people like yourself see Jesus as an imposter. But the truth is that He isn't. You can trace His lineage back through the line of David and the seed of Judah.[88] That's one of the many Jewish prophecies

88. Genesis 49:10.

about the Messiah. Jesus was a direct descendant from the house of David and the tribe of Judah. There are over three hundred Jewish prophecies telling us how to identify the Messiah. Jesus fulfilled all of them. And Grandma, He isn't the other God. There is only one God. The God who parted the Red Sea for the Israelites, guided them in the wilderness for forty years, and finally, led them into the Promised Land is the same One who died on the cross for the sins of the world. But He didn't die. He is alive! How I wish I could make you see it. But I can't, only He can."

Her Grandmother's voice became very loud. "Do you know what I think? I think you've been brainwashed. You are young and very naïve about life. It's not only the cross that is offensive to the Jewish people. There's much more. We've had to endure the persecution of the crusades and the inquisitions. And we've been called 'Christ killers.' That was taught for many years in the Catholic Church. Tell me, Becky, when did the God of the Jews have a Son? Where is that written in the Jewish Scriptures?"

Becky recalled several passages from her studies. "One

place it is mentioned is in Psalm 2:12, ESV. 'Kiss the Son lest He be angry, and you perish in the way... O blessed are all those who seek refuge and put their trust in Him!' That Psalm was written by David who, as you know, later became King of Israel.

"Another place it is written is Isaiah 7:14, ESV. Isaiah wrote, 'Therefore the Lord Himself will give you a sign; Behold the virgin shall conceive, and bear a son, and call his name Immanuel' [Literally God with us]. Isaiah was a Jewish prophet who lived about seven hundred years before Jesus was born.

"And in Isaiah 9:6, ESV, he wrote, 'For unto us a child is born, unto us a son is given, and the government shall be upon his shoulders; and his name shall be called Wonderful, Counselor, The Mighty God, The Everlasting Father, The Prince of Peace.'

"Let me ask you a question," said Becky. "Do you believe that the God of Abraham, Isaac, and Jacob promised that a Messiah would come to Earth one day?"

"Yes," said her grandmother, "the Mashiach, but He

has not come yet, and it definitely isn't Jesus."

"But Grandma, how can you be so sure? How will you be able to identify Him when He does come? Following your line of argument, when the Mashiach comes, he will be the promised Messiah of Israel. The promise was given by God in the Torah. If you accept the person who you think is the Mashiach or Messiah, you will consider yourself to be obedient to God because you accepted the One whom God sent, right? The main difference between us is that I believe the Mashiach has come, and He is Jesus. You are still waiting for the Mashiach."

Her grandmother frowned. "Going to college isn't doing much for you, is it? I always thought you were smart. I just don't understand how you can be both a Christian and a Jew. That sounds like double-talk to me."

"Yes, I am now both a Jew and a Christian. It is not double-talk. It is an irony because a Christian is someone who believes that Jesus is the promised Messiah of the Jews! The Christians simply believe Jesus is all He claimed to be. And there is a portion of Jews who always have believed and still do. They are called a 'remnant,' and I am now part of that remnant.

"Christians are not anti-Semitic or Jew haters. Because they love the Jews' Messiah, they are grateful to the Jews for giving Him to them. I've heard them say that! When a few of them met me, they have actually said to me, 'Oh, you are Jewish! Thank you for our Lord and Savior. It is through the Jewish people that He came.' Grandma, if anything, we should be jealous. They have what we could have had, but instead, we dismissed Jesus as an imposter. How sad for us and for Him because He came to the Jews—His own people—first."

Becky's grandmother thought for a while then said, "Now, you are trying to trick me. And don't think I am not going to check out those Scripture verses you quoted. And I am going to check them out in my Jewish Bible which is on my shelf at home. I don't trust the Bible they gave you in church."

"Grandma, I love you. I am not trying to deceive you, and they don't give out trick Bibles in the church either.

And please, let me say one more thing. After listening to your story, I really admire the fact that you still believe in God. Many people who have gone through what you have been through gave up on God. I read somewhere that someone who had been in a concentration camp said, 'My faith in God went up in smoke together with the smoke from the chimneys in the crematoriums.' You, however, emerged from your terrible ordeal still believing in God. I believe He will honor your faith."

She walked over to her grandmother, gave her a big hug and a kiss. "I'm going upstairs now to do some studying." She entered her room and immediately called out to Jesus, "I really need to talk to You. If You can come back now, I'd appreciate it."

A few minutes passed when the familiar swirl of colors with Jesus in the center appeared in the middle of her room.

"I was expecting to hear from you," He said. "I saw and heard the exchange between your grandmother and yourself."

"Thank You for coming back to me so quickly." Becky

hesitated a moment and looked in Jesus's face. "I have an important question to ask You. After listening to my grandmother's story, I can't help but ask—since You say You are God—why did You let the evils of Hitler and the Nazis happen?"

"That's a very good question," said Jesus, "one that's been asked often. Becky, evil has existed for a very long time, and it emanates from Satan, his minions, and the principalities and powers of darkness in which they reside. Satan has been My arch enemy for a very long time. He once was an angel, but he became jealous of Me, wanted to be like Me, and became rebellious. As a consequence, I had to expel him from heaven together with a host of his followers. He took one third of the angels with him when he left. Pride ruined him. It is the sin I hate the most.[89]

"Satan and his demonic agents live and hide now in a dark abyss. Lies and deception are their chief tools with which they try to deceive humanity. They have wrapped this world in a web of lies. His spiritual realm has great power. He was the main architect of the fall of man.

89. Isaiah 14:12.

"Creeping into the garden on his belly, disguised as a snake, he whispered lies into Eve's ear and deceived her into believing that I didn't really mean what I said when I told Adam and Eve that if the fruit of the tree of the knowledge of good and evil is eaten, they would surely die. His question to Eve, 'Did God really say that?' is the same deceptive tool he uses today making people doubt the truthfulness of My Word and the goodness of My heart. The world you see now—the sickness, the violence, the tragic accidents, the untimely deaths, the cruelty of man—are all the direct result of the fall. It's not the way I originally designed it. The heart of man after the fall, without godly influence and restraint, is wicked. It wants to do whatever it wants to do and, worse, can be controlled by evil forces and the puppet master who is Satan. [89]

"When I look down on the world now, I weep. My heart is so heavy. I know what might have been if only Adam and Eve had listened to Me. But the enemy is a master of deceit. He is always working his wiles, and the present world is in darkness and doesn't know it. He blinded them to the truth. That's why when I came to Earth and walked among them, most of the people couldn't recognize Me.[90] They had gotten used to the spiritual darkness, and their spiritually blind eyes couldn't see the light that had pierced the darkness and had come into their midst. I am the light, the truth, and the way out of the darkness which engulfs this world. That's why I often said, 'They have eyes, but they don't see.'[91]

"But Becky, you are beginning to see. Your eyes are beginning to open. Go and tell the whole world that if they will believe My words and follow Me, even now, I will lead them out of darkness into the light of a glorious new day that will grow brighter and brighter until all of the darkness is gone and the light of My presence is fully revealed."

Becky replied, "You told me that the beginning of all things was written in the first book of the Torah— Genesis. How come many Jewish people don't believe this to be literally true?"

"That's a good observation, Becky, because if the very

90. 1 Peter 5:8.
91. Mark 8:18.

foundation is not believed to be true, how can they believe that I am real? How many Jewish people really believe that there was a real Adam and Eve, and how many believe that Moses parted the Red Sea and took the Israelites across on dry land?"

"Probably not many," answered Becky. "My family thinks the story is a legend passed down by many generations." She paused then said, "So it is all literally true—there was a garden, a paradise, a man called Adam, and a woman named Eve, and Satan spoiled it all. And there was always You, just like I read in Genesis 1:1, 'In the beginning God.' Right?"

"Yes, Becky. I always was and I am."

Becky replied, "Well, this is a lot to think about. It changes everything, and I do mean everything!"

"That's what knowing the truth is meant to do," Jesus said.

"It sounds like so much of life is really a contest between You and Satan. It reminds me of a game of chess. He wants to checkmate the King. That's You."

"Yes, it can be compared to that, only life is not a game. The good news is that in the end, I win."

"I'm so grateful for that because if You win, then, I win too because I belong to You. Isn't that right?" questioned Becky.

"Yes, that's right. But let Me finish telling you what happened in Germany during that horrific time. For many years before Hitler was born, there were many atheistic philosophies which became very popular. Many German philosophers became famous and drew many people away from faith in Me. One of the most famous and influential was Friedrich Nietzsche. He wrote a piece severely criticizing Christianity and blamed all of Germany's ills on 'Christian lies.' His proclamation, 'Gott ist tot,' [God is Dead] resounds even to this day. Also, during that time, many people in Germany became fascinated with the world of the occult. The culture of atheism together with the fascination of the occult created fertile soil for all that followed. The stage was set for Hitler and the Nazi party.

"Hitler was drawn to the occult which opened him

up to its dark influences and demonic forces. He also used drugs. His mesmerizing power to sway large crowds of people came from this dark realm.

"Let Me draw you a picture of what happened in Germany. On the one hand, there is Satan. Think of a giant octopus. It has a head which controls its movements, and it also has many tentacles which enables it to function and move.

"In the same way, Satan is the head of the demonic spirit world. The occult world, the new-age cults with all its old lies, séances, the seductive drug culture, alcoholism, hypnotism, astrology, fortune-tellers, atheism, false religions, addictions, sexual perversions, pornography, and all forms of self-actualization are only some of his tentacles. This is a huge and powerful octopus.[92]

"Once the octopus grabs you with one of his tentacles, he draws you to himself. You are now under his control. He can use you or destroy you. His main objective is to keep you away from the cross and from Me. He knows that if you come to Me, you will be set free from bondage to him

92. Ephesians 6:12.

and receive everlasting life with Me. He counterfeits his offer, making it look like a good thing, but it is really a lie. It is death masquerading as life.[93]

"Politically, in the 1930s, Germany was in a state of chaos. They never recovered from their crushing defeat in World War I. Unemployment was rampant, food was scarce, and one of their most respected philosophers had told them 'God is dead.' Also, the worldwide depression of 1929 had devastating and long-lasting effects. Germany was ready for a savior.

"So onto the German stage strides Hitler empowered by the dark occult forces which have overtaken him. His well-developed megalomania and psychological weaknesses made him a choice subject to be used by Satan to achieve his purposes. Some of Hitler's fanatic followers, 'the brown shirts,' were also involved in the occult. Satan now has a perfect puppet to help fulfill his agenda and continue his harassment of the Jews. The octopus used one of his tentacles—the occult—to grab Hitler, draw him into his dark demonic world, overtake him, and use him.

93. Matthew 8:28–34.

"Everything has come together. He has Hitler, someone who wants to conquer the world. Germany, a country longing to be great again, and Germany's very weak political leadership.

"So Satan seizes the moment and strikes. He devises a diabolical plan to totally exterminate the Jews, calling them an 'inferior race.' He masterfully uses deception to appeal to the disheartened Germans and tells them that they are a superior Aryan race. It is a lie, but they believe it because they are economically, spiritually, and politically bankrupt.[94] So the Nazi flag is slowly raised toward the German sky, and the whole world watches, unaware of the monstrous evil which is about to be unleashed in the land where 'Gott ist tot.'"

"Satan seems so powerful," Becky said.

"Yes, but you don't need to be afraid of him. I am more powerful, and I am in control. He can only go as far as I allow him to go. And once you come under My protection, he will never snatch you from My hand.[95]

---

94. 1 Peter 5:8.
95. John 10:28–29.

That's a promise that I make to every believer. Satan is a seducer and a deceiver. He has deceived many people into believing he doesn't exist. Remember, the world is wrapped in spiritual darkness, and you really can't see in the dark. Without light, he can hide himself very well. He works best in the shadows."[96]

"You've been very patient with my many questions. I hope You won't be offended by my next one." Becky's tone was very cautious.

Jesus replied, "I won't be offended by anything you ask Me, Becky, because I know you are trying very hard to understand. But remember, if you want to be My follower, I ask My followers to walk by faith and not by sight.[97] Wanting to understand everything is very much like walking by sight."

"I'm not there yet. Right now, I need to understand. I'll walk by faith later."

Jesus smiled, saying, "What is your question?"

"Couldn't You have stopped the Holocaust? A lot of

---

96. 1 John 4:4; Revelation 12:9–11.
97. 2 Corinthians 5:7.

people, especially the Jewish people, don't believe in You specifically because of the Holocaust."

Jesus sighed. "Yes, I could have stopped the Holocaust. I'm sovereign and in control of the whole world. When I created Adam and Eve, I gave them free will and that included freedom to make choices. I did not create robots. Unfortunately, they made a very wrong choice when they listened to Satan instead of Me. As a result, all of their descendants, including you, inherited the legacy of a sinful nature. The consequences of their disobedience were immense. As you know now, they were expelled from the idyllic garden with severe penalties, their close relationship with Me was ruined, and I pronounced a curse on the whole Earth.

"Furthermore, their disobedience opened the door for Satan and his agents to enter and create a very destructive and evil dynamic in the world—a dynamic which had its fullest expression in the Holocaust. That was not My original plan for My creation, and My heart breaks when I think of what was and what could have been, if only. 'If only' expresses the sadness of My heart.[98]

"However, on the cross, I reversed the whole order. I paid the sin debt, removed the curse on the Earth, and I overcame Satan, his minions, and death itself. I reset the clock of creation. Now, everyone who believes in Me and sincerely accepts Me as their Savior receives a new birth, a new life, and a second chance.

"As it was in the beginning and still is, My sovereign will is to give everyone freedom of choice. In the Torah, which I wrote through My servants, I said, 'I have set before you life and death, blessings and curses; now choose life' [Deuteronomy 30:19, NIV]. You would think it would have been a simple choice, but because of their spiritual blindness, My people had eyes, but they couldn't see. Elsewhere in the Scriptures, I said, 'For whoever finds Me finds life and obtains favor from the Lord'" (Proverbs 8:35, ESV).

"So why has it been so hard for people to find You and why do You hide yourself?" asked Becky.

"It really isn't that hard, Becky. Again, in the Scriptures,

_____

98. Genesis 6:5–6.

it is written, 'You will seek Me and find Me when you seek Me with all your heart' [Jeremiah 29:13, NIV]. And I am not hiding. Look around you at the beautiful natural surroundings. All of nature declares My glory. And don't forget, in the Older Testament, I made My presence known to Moses in a burning bush and at Mt. Sinai. Also, I guided Our people in the wilderness of the desert with a cloud by day and a pillar of fire at night. In the tabernacle, in the wilderness, and in Solomon's temple, I appeared as the Shekinah Glory, and finally, in the Newer Testament, I appeared in person—in the flesh. Anyone who sincerely wants to find Me will find Me. I'm just a prayer away. Becky, you asked Me a lot of questions. But there is one question you haven't asked Me."[99]

"What is that?"

"You haven't asked Me why I died for you."

Becky thought for a few minutes, then said, "Oh, I thought You told me why."

"I did," said Jesus, "but in relation to the questions you've been asking—some of which points to the injustices

99. Acts 17:27–28.

in life—I want you to focus on Me. I was innocent, but I died for the guilty. If you will think about that for a while, it will redirect your thoughts and change your heart and your grandmother's heart as well. I am not trivializing the impact of life's negative experiences or the wounding that comes from them. I am pointing out that the gift of salvation overrules everything in this life and offers you a relationship with someone strong who comes alongside you and helps you overcome. The negative experiences in life are, sometimes, very powerful and can be similar to the ocean's undercurrent or riptide which can suck you under the waves. I know what once happened to you in the ocean when you were a young girl. Do you remember? I was there. That's why you weren't pulled out to sea."[100]

Becky's mind went back to that very terrifying episode. "Yes, I remember that. I was so scared! But the current changed suddenly, and I was able to swim safely toward shore. So are You saying that if I experience something very negative, unjust, or unfair, I shouldn't dwell on it for too long but, instead, focus on the fact that the gift of salvation

100. Matthew 8:27.

is totally undeserved and overrules everything—the good, the bad, and the ugly?"[101]

Jesus nodded. "Yes, if you feel overwhelmed with a negative experience, ask yourself, 'Why did I die for you?' I was innocent, and you were the guilty one. That will redirect your thoughts. What you receive from Me now and throughout all eternity more than makes up for anything you may lose or suffer in this life. First, you will receive My forgiveness which will enable you to have a restored relationship with Me. Only the forgiven can enter the kingdom of God. Secondly, your life will be cleansed and renewed, and you will receive the gift of My Holy Spirit which will come to live within you. My Holy Spirit will enable you to live a fruitful and abundant life which includes the privilege of leading others into My kingdom.[102]

"The door to heaven will be opened to you, and it is there you will live with Me and My other children forever and ever. It is written, 'What no eye has seen, nor ear heard, nor the heart of man imagined, what God has prepared for

---

101. Cp Jonah 1:17, 4:6–8.
102. Galatians 5:16.

those who love Him' [1 Corinthians 2:9, ESV]. You can't even imagine what is waiting for you when you step onto heaven's shores.

"In addition, Becky, I died for you because I love you, and I want you and everyone who believes in Me to have a close relationship with Me during your temporary life on Earth and throughout eternity in heaven. This is possible only through My death on the cross which paid the debt you owed for your sin. When you accept Me as your Savior, I promise to be with you during your life's journey, guiding and guarding your steps and meeting all of your needs according to My purpose for your life. I will be your refuge in times of trouble, your shield against the darts of your enemies, and your ally in times of strong opposition. When you are weak, I will be your strength, and when you are discouraged, I will be your song. With your new birth, you enter into a relationship with Me and receive a new life. I will never fail you, Becky. So come and follow Me. We have work to do.[103]

"I have to leave now, but I'll be back again. We are

103. John 3:16–17.

making progress. You are a good listener. Write down all that I have told you, and I will show you how to cast your net into the sea. We are going fishing."

Chapter 10

Becky was in the midst of making plans to go to the Hebrew University in Israel when her father became ill. He was diagnosed with cancer and was hospitalized. The doctors told her mother that he only had about a year or a year and a half to live. The next Sunday, Becky went to a nearby church to pray. There, she met a Jewish-Christian named Miriam. She had met her once before.

Becky told her about her father's illness. Miriam suggested that Becky send someone to the hospital to share the Gospel with him, and she recommended a certain Jewish-Christian pastor from upstate New York, Pastor

Isaac. Becky remembered meeting him at the performance of "The Tribunal." He was warm and friendly. She said to Miriam, "That's a good idea, but I think I'll wait a while. My mother and brother, Charlie, don't know the Lord either, so if I wait until my father comes home from his treatment at the hospital, all three of them can hear the Gospel."

Miriam responded very emphatically, "No, Becky, what does the Bible say? It says, 'Now is the day of salvation' [2 Corinthians 6:2, NIV]. Don't wait."

Thinking about what Miriam said, Becky rose from her seat and walked toward the front door of the church. On her way out, she accidently bumped into a man. Quite to her surprise, it was Pastor Isaac. He greeted Becky and told her that he was in town for a week for some appointments.

Becky asked him if he had a moment to talk to her. She took him aside and told him about her father's illness. She also told him about her plan to wait until her father came home, but the pastor, like Miriam, strongly suggested that she not wait, volunteering to visit her father while he was in the hospital. He asked, "Is your father open to hearing about the Gospel?"

"I don't think so," Becky replied. "But I plan to visit him this afternoon, so I'll let you know for sure."

Becky and Pastor Isaac exchanged phone numbers.

"Now that your father is ill," said Pastor Isaac, "he might be more receptive. Be sure to tell him that I am Jewish, so he will feel more comfortable."

CHAPTER 11

Becky visited her father in the hospital. She was not quite sure what to expect or what to say.

"Hi, Dad, how are you feeling today?" She tried to sound upbeat.

"Not too good," said her father. "But they are giving me radiation treatments, and the doctor says they'll know more by next week."

"Look, Dad," said Becky, "I know you are not happy about my involvement with the church and Jesus, but as you know, life is very challenging at times. We can't go through these difficult experiences alone, and we don't have to. Dad, trust me, Jesus can help you. Would you be willing to listen to someone who is a Jewish-Christian? He's a pastor who lives upstate, and he's visiting Brooklyn right now. Quite frankly, I don't think it was a coincidence that I just happened to bump into him today. I think this is a 'God moment.'"

Her father looked intently at her. "Becky, I know that I am very ill, and life is much bigger than I can comprehend with my finite mind. I know, too, that something very dramatic has happened to you, even though I can't understand it. I've been doing a lot of thinking lately. I don't have much to do these days, lying in bed all day. I think it will be okay if he visits me. I will listen to whatever he has to say." He grinned, adding, "And I promise to behave myself and not throw the water pitcher at him."

"Good," said Becky. "Do you want to pray?" She expected her father to say no, but quite to her surprise, he said okay. Moving the chair closer to him, she took his hands in hers and said, "Just listen to what I am saying. You don't have to say anything right now." Becky began to pray,

"Oh, Heavenly Father, I thank You for my salvation. You are the only true and living God, and there is no other. Thank You for sending Your only Son, Yeshua, who is also called Jesus to Earth to die for our sins. You know how difficult it is for us, as Jewish people, to accept Jesus as the Messiah. Everything is all mixed up. You sent Him to us first, but we couldn't see clearly and rejected Him. We thought He was an imposter. However, because You are a loving and forgiving God, You are giving me and every Jewish person another chance. I am now part of the believing remnant of Jewish people You speak of in the Holy Scriptures. Here I am, at my father's bedside. He is very ill. I pray for him, dear Jesus. Please open his eyes and reveal Yourself to him as his Messiah too. The Bible, which You wrote, says that all of us have only a certain amount of days to live here on Earth. Death closes the final chapter of our lives. 'Man's days are numbered' [Job 14:5, NLV]. Those are Your exact words. So dear Lord, I intercede on my father's behalf." Becky squeezed her father's hands and continued, "I place his hands in Your hands, Jesus, and I pray that You will be merciful to him. Open the eyes of his understanding so he can see You clearly. I pray this in Your name. Amen."

Becky looked at her father. "It isn't very complicated. When you are alone tonight, just ask God if He had a Son and if His name is Yeshua. That's His Hebrew name. God will answer you. He is always listening. Then, if you feel God is guiding you, just ask Him into your heart. That's all it takes. A sincere and open heart. As I think you know, Jesus died between two thieves. One accepted Him, and the other didn't. The one who accepted Him only spoke a few words. He said, 'Jesus, remember me when You come into Your kingdom.' Jesus answered him, 'Truly I say to you, today you will be with Me in paradise'" (Luke 23:42–43, ESV).

"Becky, I never knew you could be this persistent. However, I listened to every word you said. I never heard you pray before. Something has definitely happened to you. That much I know. I know too that I am in a precarious situation. Cancer is a formidable foe, and I need more than medicine and radiation treatments to overcome it. I will talk to God tonight as you suggest."

Becky kissed his forehead and said, "I will come back in a few days." She closed the door, walked down the hospital corridor, and whispered, "Oh, Jesus, please save him."

When Becky returned home, she called Pastor Isaac and told him about her visit to her father and gave him the address of the hospital.

Since she had been told that her father had about a year or a year and a half to live, she thought she could continue her preparations for her trip to Israel. *Sometimes, people live longer than their doctor's prognosis, and he really didn't look that bad,* she thought.

Becky's relationship with her mother had become distant, mainly because her mother was focused on Becky's father's illness, and she couldn't deal with Becky's newfound faith in Jesus. Becky and her mother had always been close, and they loved each other very much, so this was very difficult for both of them.

Her grandmother wasn't talking to her. During her

frequent visits, she treated Becky like someone who had joined the Nazi party. Her brother, Charles, taunted her by being sarcastic. Sometimes, he would greet her by saying, "Well, look who's here. The *goy* [Gentile] is home." But Becky loved them anyway.

Becky managed to deal with all of this by frequently praying for strength and wisdom. Her anchor was that she was convinced that God was guiding her; that Jesus was indeed the Messiah, and the prospect of going to Israel in a few weeks filled her with joy. She couldn't wait to visit the places she had read about in the Bible and, especially, to walk the same roads Jesus had walked.

A few days later, she received a phone call from Pastor Isaac. He had visited her father in the hospital and said, "Becky, your father didn't accept Jesus, but his heart was very tender toward Him. I shared the Gospel with him, he listened, and God will do the rest. It's in His hands."

Becky was disappointed but consoled herself with the thought that there still was a lot more time left. She visited her father again, prayed with him, and reminded him to talk and pray to God before he went to sleep. Once again, he said he would.

CHAPTER 12

The next day, a little before noon, the phone rang. She picked it up and heard the doctor's voice. "Becky, I have some very bad news. Your father passed away early this morning."

Becky couldn't believe it. She blurted out, "But I thought he had much more time."

The doctor said, "I'm very sorry, his heart wasn't strong enough to handle the radiation. Please let your family know and ask your mother to call me. We need to make some arrangements."

Becky hung up the phone, began to cry, and suddenly

remembered what Miriam had said to her in church just a week ago. "Don't wait. The Bible says, 'Now is the day of salvation.'" Becky was grateful she had listened to her, and then, she began to put the pieces together. Her timely meeting with Miriam, "accidentally bumping" into Pastor Isaac upon leaving the church that very afternoon, and the pastor's visit to her father. Even her father being willing to listen and pray was unusual. Then, as she thought about these events, she realized that God had arranged it all. He knew that her father didn't have a year or a year and a half to live as the doctor had told her. He only had one week. Becky thought, *I only hope he accepted Jesus before he died. That's all that counts.* She heard the key in the front door and voices. Her mother and Charlie were home.

Becky shared the news with them. They all cried. Funeral arrangements were made. The only encouraging moment during this period was a dream that Becky had a few days after her father had died. She dreamed that her father came to her and told her, "I did what you told me to do." She was greatly comforted by this.

After the funeral, Becky completed the final arrangements for her trip. She postponed her departure date, so she could spend some time with her mother, brother Charlie, and grandmother. Her father's death had deeply affected all of them. Her grandmother had moved into the house. Charlie grew increasingly depressed. He missed his father and was very upset about Becky's plan to be a Christian missionary in Israel. For some reason, Becky's decision to follow Jesus challenged Charlie's identity as a Jew.

Sheldon, Charlie's close friend, was planning to go to Israel and visit his brother who lived there, and he invited Charlie to join him. He said, "Getting away from everything might help you gain some perspective." Charlie agreed and bought an airline ticket. In the meantime, as he waited for his departure date, he spent time alone in his room surfing the internet. Then, after a few days, he said goodbye and left. Becky, her mother, and grandmother didn't know what to think or say, so they let him go without an argument. They hoped the trip would help him.

Soon, it was time for Becky to leave for Israel. She had

already contacted the Hebrew University in Israel and was connected with someone there who said they would help her find an inexpensive apartment nearby and get settled. She did not disclose that she was a Jewish-Christian.

When it was time for Becky to leave, it was a very awkward and tense moment. She said goodbye to her mother and grandmother. There were tears in everyone's eyes as they hugged each other. As a family, they had shared a lot together, and they loved each other very much in spite of everything that had happened. Becky's mother and grandmother were hoping that this was a phase Becky was going through, and she would return home soon. Becky, however, knew differently.

Her friend, Barbara, arrived to take Becky to the airport. The drive would give both of them some quality time together before Becky's plane departed. Becky placed her suitcases in Barbara's car and waved a final goodbye. As they headed to the airport, Becky and Barbara talked about the recent events.

"Boy, things certainly have changed and fast," said

Barbara. "One day, we were seated next to each other in the school cafeteria, and now, here I am driving you to the airport for your trip to Israel."

"It has been very sudden, and the events have not only been fast moving, but very surprising," said Becky. "Barbara, I'm so glad we are friends. I hope we remain so. You have been so helpful to me, mainly because you have an open mind. You think outside the box and have helped me not only to do so as well but also to be strong. Otherwise, I wouldn't be sitting here." Becky sat silent for a few minutes.

Barbara said in a reassuring tone, "I value our friendship as well and hope we will keep in touch and always be friends. I will check in with your mother and grandmother from time to time to make sure they are okay."

Becky said, "You know, I am worried about Charlie. He seems very disappointed in me and somewhat angry. I think my grandmother has influenced him. A few days ago, when no one was home, I was wandering through the house just to take some of the memories with me. I walked into Charlie's room and on his desk was a copy of an online application for the Israeli Air Force. It looked like he had printed it off the internet. I was very surprised. He hadn't mentioned this to me or my mother before he left. I read something he wrote on the application form. It was an affirmation of his being a Jew. He ended it by stating that he categorically rejects the idea of Jesus being the Jewish Messiah. They didn't ask him that question." Becky sighed. "It's so hard to explain to people that I have not turned my back on the Jewish people. I have simply accepted our Messiah."

"I know, and I understand," said Barbara. "My parents are not too keen about my being involved with yoga and having a guru from India. I can't imagine what would happen if I told them that I, too, think Jesus is the Messiah of Israel."

"You do?" responded Becky.

"Yes, I've been reading the Bible too, and something very unusual is really going on here with you. But I am not ready to take that step and leap of faith just now. It's really sad when you think about it. Jesus suffered so much, and all He was trying to do was to save people. I guess that's why on the cross He said, 'Father, forgive them, for they do not know what they are doing'" (Luke 23:34, NIV).

"All of us are in different places on our journey in life," Becky replied. "By the way," she continued, "I forgot to tell you the dream I had the other night. It was a beautiful sunny day, and I was outdoors. I raised my arm and stretched it all the way toward the sky. My hand reached into the clouds and pulled down a white index card. On it was written one word 'Reuben.'

"The first thought that came to me was a Reuben sandwich. But then, I thought, 'What does that have to do with anything? So I looked for the meaning of the name in the Bible. It is a Hebrew word. Do you know what it means?"

"No," Barbara answered.

Becky said, "The name Reuben literally means, 'See, a Son.'"

"Wow, that's cool!" Barbara replied. They both were silent for a little while.

"So when you arrive in Israel, what is your plan?" asked Barbara.

Becky looked at her check list. "I have several names of churches and people to contact. The first thing I have to do is find an apartment near the university. I spoke to someone who is going to help me find one. Then, I'll check out a few churches and wait to hear from Jesus about the next step."

Barbara frowned. "Our people will look upon you as a turncoat—a traitor. Are you up for that?"

"I'm not sure. The most important thing is to help the Jewish people understand that Jesus is the long-promised Messiah of Israel and that the gift He is offering is immense and eternal. Where we spend eternity is the most important thing. And that is decided here on this side. If I can help in some small way, then, my life will have meaning. I believe God has a plan for my life. Otherwise, He wouldn't have visited me."

"What do you think His plan is?" Barbara asked. "He told me we were going fishing."

"Fishing?"

"I think He meant fishing for souls," answered Becky.

They drove and talked some more, and then, suddenly, the signs to the airport appeared. When they reached the departure terminal, a porter helped take the bags to the nearby check-in station.

With tears in their eyes, they hugged each other and said goodbye. Barbara said, "Go with God. I will miss you, dear friend."

As Becky walked through the terminal, she became a little apprehensive. *I really hope I am doing the right thing,* she thought. She paused and checked her pocketbook and looked over the names of the churches in Israel which had been recommended to her and the names of people to contact there.

Then, feeling a little better, she continued walking to the departure gate, saw the check-in desk, and presented her passport and ticket. Everything seemed to be in order, so she was given her boarding pass. Suddenly, she felt very hungry. Spotting a nearby coffee bar, Becky hurried over and ordered coffee and a bagel with cream cheese. She smiled and thought, *I wonder if the bagels in Israel will be this good.*

After eating, she returned to the lounge near the departure gate, sat down, and opened her Bible. She read and prayed silently, *Jesus, please guide my steps, protect me from all harm, and land me safely in Jerusalem.*

When the announcement came that the plane was ready to be boarded, Becky rose from her seat, took a deep breath, and walked forward to the gate. She handed the agent her boarding pass, walked down the ramp, entered the plane, found her seat and sat down. Becky had always been afraid of flying, but now, she felt unusually calm. She knew that it was God's peace. He was with her. She no longer felt afraid or alone.

The takeoff was smooth, so she relaxed, pushed her seat back, and took out her Bible. It had become her constant companion through these days, especially since the death of her father and the conflicts in her family. She opened the Bible and began to read the Scriptures written by the prophet Jeremiah.

She read Jeremiah 2:5, NIV, "What fault did your ancestors find in Me, that they strayed so far from Me?" She was startled and almost said out loud, "Oh, my goodness. These are almost the same words my parents said to me when I told them I had accepted Jesus!" She remembered they asked her, "How did we fail you?"

Now, for the first time, she understood that God had feelings and could be hurt. Through the Jewish prophet, Jeremiah, God was speaking to the Israelites just like a parent would to his children. He was asking them how He had failed them and caused them to turn from Him.

Becky remembered how wounded her parents were, and she thought to herself, *God must have felt the same way when His people—the Israelites—turned their back on Him and His ways.* Becky's eyes filled with tears as she vividly remembered the scene with her parents at the breakfast table. Of course, she reminded herself, *I didn't turn my back on them and my Jewish heritage, but they thought I did.*

The flight to Jerusalem was relatively calm, so she

closed the Bible, pushed back her seat, wiped the tears from her eyes, and dozed off.

Becky awoke to the clattering noise of the food trays being handed out by the flight attendants. She wondered what was being served. The aroma was wonderful. She put her seat in the upright position and gratefully took the food tray that was handed to her. "Boy, I'm really hungry," she said to the man sitting beside her.

He answered, "Yes, I'm hungry too. I noticed you were reading a Bible a little while ago. Do you believe in God?"

"Yes, I do." Becky didn't want to identify herself as a Jewish-Christian because that would take too much time to explain, and she really wanted to eat.

He introduced himself as Dr. Gordon Joseph and told Becky that he was a medical doctor on his way home for a visit with his family. Becky smiled inwardly, thinking how happy her mother would be to learn that she had met a Jewish doctor!

They began to chat, and Dr. Joseph said, "I'm curious about people who believe in the Bible. Do you believe in evolution or creation?"

"I believe in creation," Becky said. "I believe it happened just the way God said it did."

"Really!" He looked at her with a somewhat condescending smile. "So you believe there was a real Garden of Eden and a man called Adam and a woman called Eve?

Becky strongly affirmed, "Yes, I do."

"You do know that scientific evidence supports the theory of evolution more than the story of creation."

"I'm not so sure it does," said Becky. "Evolution is just a theory. As for scientific facts, the Bible has many. Did you know that Isaiah—a Jewish prophet who lived around seven hundred years before the birth of Jesus— described the Earth as a circle? Speaking of God, the Scriptures say, 'He sits enthroned above the *circle* of the Earth, and its people are like grasshoppers. He stretches out the heavens like a canopy and spreads them out like a tent to live in.' [Isaiah 40:22, NIV].

"The popular belief at that time was that the Earth

was flat. Even the Israelites believed that the Earth was a flat disc floating on water beneath an arched firmament separating it from the heavens. Who told Isaiah that the Earth was round and not flat?"

Dr. Joseph's interest was piqued. He put his fork down and waited to hear more. "I never heard that."

"And here's another interesting scientific fact, the exact dimensions of Noah's Ark were described in detail. When the rains came, Genesis says the waters rose to a depth of more than twenty feet over the mountains. That amount of water was sufficient to safely carry Noah, his family, and his precious cargo over the highest mountaintop. If it had rained less, the boat would have crashed into the mountain, and we wouldn't be sitting here talking to each other."

"Well, I'm intrigued now and will certainly check all this out when I get home."

"There's more. Do you mind if I continue?"

Dr. Joseph said, "Not at all. I find this conversation very intriguing."

Becky continued, "As you said, the theory of evolution

is just that—a theory. Some people have a problem believing in creationism because of the number of animals supposed to be on Noah's ark. Well, I heard about another theory and it is this. Two of every kind, not two of every species were on board the ark. For example, when two dogs left the ark, they left with a genetic pool of information which emerged over time as many different species. But these species always were of the same kind and referred back to the two original dogs. Cats were never in the genetic pool of dogs and vice versa. God's creation always reproduces after its own kind. It's the same with us. Noah left the ark with the genetic pool of humanity, and we are all part of that same human genetic pool. Different colors of skin stems from different pigmentation. But every human being is from the same generic pool of humanity and reproduces after its own kind. *And* do you know what that means?"

Dr. Joseph, listening intently, replied, "No, I don't."

"It means that humans were never in the same genetic pool of monkeys and apes, and monkeys were never in the genetic pool of humans! I think Darwin misinterpreted the genetic pools and called it evolution."

By this time, the people seated around Becky and Dr. Joseph were fully engaged in listening to their conversation. No one was eating.

"Do you want to hear one more?" she said.

Dr. Joseph folded his hands. "Go for it. You have my full attention." Looking around, he added, "And I think everyone else's!"

"I think you will appreciate this one, particularly because you are a physician. In Leviticus 15:13, God instructs the Israelites to wash their garments and themselves in 'running water' [KJV]. This was many, many years before Louis Pasteur and his theory of germs and disease. The microscope and the cause of infectious diseases were unknown. But God knew!"

"I didn't know that."

"I didn't know any of this either until I began to study. That's why it is so important to get all of the facts before we dismiss something as we all sometimes do. I have learned that science and the Bible are not incompatible. Science relies on verification and proving that the evidence which is being examined is true. Nothing can be more truthful than God's Word. The problem is we, as a secular society, have held up the evidence of science as being true and dismissed the Bible as being false or fiction. Why have we done that? Because I think we want to be in control, and we can't be in control of something we don't fully understand. Everything has to be subject to our understanding. Those of us who think that way have placed man as the measure and center of all things. Self is on the throne and, in essence, we've told God to take a hike."

Becky continued, "Science demands that facts be verified, but these facts are confined to a limited time and space continuum. They're also limited to what our finite minds can comprehend. What we can see, touch, feel, smell, and taste is considered by some to be all there is to life. The Bible values verification of facts as well, but it also embraces a larger field which includes another dimension—one that is equally true, although much more difficult to prove. There is a spiritual world that transcends the physical one. And it is accessed by faith."

As Becky was speaking, she felt a surge of energy throughout her whole body, and her mind felt unusually sharp. She remembered that Jesus told her that He would fill her with His Holy Spirit and enable her to speak with authority and clarity. She knew that this wasn't her usual self speaking. Something or someone was guiding her words. They just flowed out of her effortlessly.

"I don't believe the state of the world can be explained by the theory of evolution. According to that theory, everything is progressing and advancing to the next higher level. You only have to turn on the TV or read a newspaper to know that civilization is not moving upward. We did not begin at the bottom and work our way upward. No, we started at the top and fell to the bottom. Evolution does not offer any hope to mankind. Are things getting better? No, they are not. And they won't get better. There is only one hope and that is God and, specifically, the offer of salvation through His only Son, Jesus Christ."

Becky forgot about her meal for the moment. She

continued, "Let me give you another example. In the Older Testament, there were more than three hundred prophecies describing the coming of a Messiah or Mashiach. Many of them have literally been fulfilled and point to Jesus. Some of them were written hundreds and hundreds of years before the actual events took place. How can that be explained?"

Dr. Joseph was impressed but puzzled. "Boy, you really have done your homework. Are you a Jew or a Christian?"

"I am both," she said. Now, almost finished with her meal, she explained what that meant.

He smiled. "You are really deep into this, aren't you?"

"I had to pour myself into all of this and get my facts straight because it cost me a lot to travel on this path. I shed a lot of tears. But there was joy as well. The joy of discovery. As someone who reveres science, I'm sure you can appreciate that."

"You know, I consider myself committed to my profession and beliefs," said Dr. Joseph. "But I can't say that I ever cried over them."

Becky and Dr. Joseph finished eating their dinner, and then, he said, "Why don't we lighten the rest of our trip and watch a movie."

Becky agreed, and they both turned on the movie channel.

After the movie, Becky and Dr. Joseph asked for some soda and snacks and continued talking. "I've been thinking," she said. "You are not a believer, are you?"

"If I had to define myself spiritually, I would say I am an agnostic. With regard to God, 'the jury is still out' in my mind," said Dr. Joseph. "What are you thinking?"

"Well, you are a medical doctor. How can you look at the marvel of the human body and not believe that there is a designer? Take the eye for example. It's a miracle of design, functioning just like a camera."

"Yes, the human body is a wonder," he admitted. "But is it God's design or just part of the evolutionary process?"

"Well, I cast my vote for God!" Becky's voice was firm.

Their conversation was interrupted by the flight attendant asking everyone to fasten their seatbelts. They were approaching their destination. Becky could feel her heart begin to beat faster as they began the descent. *We're almost here*, she thought. "Israel! I've only seen pictures of it." After a little while, from her window seat, she could see the topography of the land. No tall buildings, just mountains and desert.

As the plane continued its descent, Becky began to see signs of civilization. Small buildings and then some taller ones came into view. On one particular building she saw several large familiar blue and white flags of Israel billowing in the breeze.

With a lump in her throat and tears in her eyes, she turned to Dr. Joseph and said, "I feel like I've come home."

The plane made a smooth landing at the Ben Gurion Airport in Tel Aviv. Becky and Dr. Joseph retrieved their carry-on baggage and exited the plane. After going through customs, they followed the line moving toward the street. On the sidewalk, they exchanged phone numbers and said goodbye. Both said how much they had enjoyed each other's company and promised to keep in touch.

Becky hailed a taxi, and the driver helped her place her

luggage in the car. The drive to Jerusalem was a little more than an hour. She relaxed in the back seat of the car and reviewed in her mind her conversation with Dr. Joseph. Becky thought about him for a little while, reflecting upon his openness to listen to her viewpoint and how attractive he was. Then, she looked out of the window and watched the passing scenery. *It's definitely different from Brooklyn!* she thought. From her window, she could see the various shops and the diversity of people, some wearing colorful Middle Eastern garments. With the window open, every once in a while, she could smell the aroma of freshly cooked food. *I'm really here*, she thought.

As the taxi approached Jerusalem, she told the driver the address of one of her contacts there. She called ahead to let her hosts know of her arrival.

Now, she was really excited! She began to see the walls of the old city, and the historical significance of being in Jerusalem began to sink in. She thought about the Bible, the history of her people, the Jews, and especially, Jesus—how He actually had been here. The old city looked different then, but this was the location where He lived. Now, I will be able to walk almost in the same places where He walked. She spied the mountains in the distance and thought about how they probably hadn't changed much and certainly hadn't moved! Jesus had looked at those same mountains! She made a mental note that one of her first visits would be to the Temple Mount and the Sea of Galilee. She began to make a list of other places she wanted to visit.

"We are almost there," said the taxi driver.

She prayed silently, *Lord, please watch over me, protect me, guide me, and give me eyes that see, ears that hear, and a teachable spirit. Please don't let me miss any opportunity You have prepared for me. I am so grateful to You, not only for my salvation but for the privilege of sharing my faith in You with our people. Please give me the wisdom, strength, and courage to be Your instrument of peace. I love You, Jesus. Amen.*

CHAPTER 13

Becky was welcomed by her hosts, Gloria and Roger. They were looking forward to her arrival. After taking her to her freshly prepared room, they got acquainted with each other over dinner. Afterward, alone in her room, Becky unpacked her bags and again thought, *I can't really believe I am here.*

She looked out of her window, saw the lights of Jerusalem, and quietly thanked God for her safe arrival. After changing into her pajamas, she picked up her Bible, and read a few of the Psalms.

Suddenly, the familiar circle of colors appeared in the

room. It was Jesus, and He said, "I'm so glad you are here, Becky. I know it was difficult to leave your family, especially so soon after your father died, but your future is here now."

"Do You mind if I ask You a question? If my future is here now, why wasn't I born here, and why wasn't I born into a Christian family? Everything would have been much simpler that way," said Becky as she stared into His face.

"My ways and thoughts are not your ways, Becky," Jesus answered. "You have to trust Me. Tomorrow is Sunday. Roger and Gloria will take you to a Messianic Church nearby, and there, you will meet some other Jewish believers. Then, you won't feel quite so alone.[104]

"On Monday, you can register at the Hebrew University. I will guide your steps, Becky. Don't be afraid. Please remember, I love you." The swirl of colors slowly receded, and He was gone. Becky closed her Bible and drifted off into a restful sleep.

When the next day dawned, Becky showered, dressed, and went downstairs. The dining room table looked like a banquet—there were bagels, all kinds of cheeses, a variety

104. Isaiah 55:8–9.

of cooked fish, and fruits all beautifully arranged. She greeted Gloria and Roger and gratefully sat down to enjoy the sumptuous breakfast.

She shared with Roger and Gloria some of the difficulties she had encountered with her family because of Jesus. She asked them where the main air force base was because she wanted to get in touch with Charlie. She also shared with them the visits from Jesus. They seem surprised but accepted her story as real. In fact, Gloria said, "Some people won't believe you, Becky, but God is God, and He can do whatever He wants. Roger and I didn't come to faith in that way. We came to faith by regularly attending church and reading the Bible."

They told her that the negative experiences she experienced with her family were not unusual. Then, they shared the challenges which they had to face and overcome. Roger said, "Just trust Jesus. Rest in His faithfulness. He won't fail you." They finished their meal and prepared to go to church.

Becky, Gloria, and Roger arrived at the Messianic

Church and found a place to sit. Becky looked around and noticed the Jewish symbols. Carved into the front of the wooden pulpit was the Star of David with a cross inside of it. On one side of the platform was a large Israeli flag; on the other side was another flag with a cross on it. On the walls were paintings of biblical scenes—Daniel in the lion's den, Moses with his raised arm holding a long staff as the Red Sea parts in front of him, and one of Jesus, seated on a hill, speaking to the multitudes in front of Him. The sanctuary itself was large and almost full of people. Becky told Gloria that she was surprised at the number of people who were in the room. Gloria replied, "Sunday services are usually well-attended and most of them are Jews."

Becky reached for a pew Bible and opened it. It contained both the Older and Newer Testaments. Becky remembered what Jesus had told her, "It's really one book. One story. One author. It's God's story of His redeeming love and grace. It begins in the first book of the Torah, Genesis with paradise lost, and ends in the last book of the Bible, Revelation with paradise regained."

It all happened right here in Israel. And now, I'm here, she thought.

A small group singing and playing musical instruments opened the service. They sang both Christian and Jewish songs. The Jewish melodies reminded Becky of home, and her eyes began to fill with tears.

When the music ended, the pastor climbed the platform stairs and warmly welcomed the congregation. He opened the Bible and read a passage from the Scriptures. His sermon topic was "Slaying the Giants in Your Life," and he named some of them— fear, anger, jealousy, greed, addictions, etc. Using the story of David and Goliath as an illustration, he said, "David didn't need to know Goliath's strength because He already knew God's."

It was a dynamic sermon. When it was over, Becky felt renewed and spiritually refreshed. The service ended with some more worshipful singing.

Coffee and a variety of desserts were served in a large room underneath the sanctuary. Gloria and Roger introduced Becky to some of their friends, and Becky began to feel more comfortable and relaxed. "I think I will be happy here," she told them.

After the service, they offered to take Becky on a tour of the neighborhood. Becky asked them if they could take her to see the Wailing Wall.

When they arrived at the wall, the area was dense with visitors. Some very orthodox Jews were standing or sitting in chairs in front of the wall fervently praying, so it was difficult to approach too closely. They slowly and respectfully pushed their way forward. Becky took some paper out of her bag and wrote something on it. Then, she managed to squeeze herself through to the front and pushed the piece of paper into one of the cracks in the wall. She stepped back and prayed for a few minutes. She told Roger and Gloria that she placed the names of her mother, brother, and grandmother on the paper and prayed for their salvation.

Becky took another step back and took in the scene, a picture she had seen many, many times on television. She was very impressed with the number of people, mostly

Jews, who were sincerely praying. The sound of their voices, rising in a rhythmic chant, warmed her heart. *The Wailing Wall! It's been here for thousands of years, and I was able to actually touch it. If those stones could talk, maybe they would say they saw Jesus pass by one day*, she thought.

After their visit to the Wailing Wall, Becky, Gloria, and Roger returned to the apartment. Becky was anxious to speak to Charlie who had arrived in Israel a month prior to her arrival. Just before she left New York, she learned that he had joined the Israeli Air Force. She wanted to know why. Not only was this sudden and unexpected, but in her mind, it was irrational and so unlike Charlie. Gloria and Roger helped Becky locate the air force base where Charlie was stationed. She called him and, after they talked for a few minutes, arranged to meet the next day.

After she hung up, Becky felt tired. It had been a long day, and she still felt some jet lag. She thought, *Tomorrow is going to be a very busy day for me. I'm going to register at the Hebrew University and then see Charlie. I think I better turn in.*

Thanking her hosts for their hospitality and a wonderful day, she went upstairs to her room, praying for a good night's sleep.

When she awoke early the next day, feeling fully rested, she thanked God and read some of the Psalms as part of her morning devotions. She was really excited to be in Israel. She got dressed, went downstairs, and had breakfast with Gloria and Roger. Gloria offered to drive Becky to the Hebrew University.

Chapter 14

In the car on the way to the university, Gloria and Becky had a chance to chat and bond a little with each other. Soon, the university appeared. Gloria parked her car, and she and Becky walked toward the registration office. Becky looked for her college transfer papers in her tote bag.

The registration process went much smoother than anticipated, and Gloria and Becky were soon back in the car, on their way to see Charlie. Becky told Gloria how grateful she was for her help and company. As they headed toward the air force base, Becky could feel herself becoming anxious. She asked Gloria to pull over to the side of the road where they prayed for God's peace.

The air force base became visible in the distance, and the car soon arrived at the entrance checkpoint. Becky told the officer that she was visiting her brother. He had left her name at the gate, so the car was permitted to enter the base. They found the parking lot, and Gloria asked, "Shall I stay and wait for you here, or do you want me to come back for you later. Either way is fine with me."

Becky replied, "You mentioned you have some errands to do. If you don't mind, why don't you do them and come back for me in about three hours. I'll be fine here on the base. I'm not sure what kind of reception I'm going to get from Charlie, and if he sees you, he will probably assume that you are one of my co-conspirators, so it might make it more difficult. Is that okay with you?"

"No problem," said Gloria. "I completely understand. I had to go through similar maneuvers with my family as well. Just think of it, we are 'partners in crime!' Only the crime is sharing the love of Jesus," Gloria replied with a grin.

Becky and Gloria said goodbye, and Becky walked toward the main office. She was now extremely apprehensive and said a prayer as she walked. Charlie was her brother, and she knew that he loved her, but he was also angry at her. *Imagine doing something like this! What was he thinking?* she thought.

She entered the office and immediately saw Charlie waiting for her. They greeted each other with a cordial hug, and then, Charlie led her to the chapel on the base, so they could talk privately. It was quiet in the chapel, and no one was there. They sat down and began to talk.

Becky could barely contain herself, "Why did you do this? What were you thinking?"

"After Dad died and you decided to become a Christian missionary, I felt kind of alone and lost. Also, I was very angry with you for turning your back on the Jewish people."

Becky interrupted him. "If I hear that one more time, I'm going to scream! That's not what happened, I did not turn my back on our people. Jesus is the Messiah of Israel, and our people have turned their backs on Him."

Charlie looked straight into her eyes. "That's not how most Jewish people see it. However, the main reason I joined the Israeli Air Force was because I wanted to experience something entirely new and different. I felt it would ease my pain after Dad died. I also believed fighting to protect Israel and the Jewish people would give my life both meaning and purpose. And it does!"

Becky leaned back against the bench. "So here we are, more than five thousand miles from home, in Israel. I think we are really here for the same reason. You just said that because of your love for the Jewish people, you want to protect them. Well, because of my love for them, I want to reintroduce them to their Messiah. He's someone who can protect them more than any armed forces can."

"Let me ask you a question, Becky. How come you were given this special revelation while the rest of us are left in the dark?"

"I'm not special, Charlie, and I don't know why Jesus came to me." They sat quietly for a while in the chapel, talked some more about home and their mutual friends, and then, Charlie asked Becky if she wanted to have some lunch. He had a pass to leave the base for a few hours. They left the chapel and headed for a nearby café.

During lunch, Charlie said, "You know, Becky, I went to Hebrew school too. I am familiar with the story of creation. God, we are told, created everything there is. That means He created the angels. Since the devil is a fallen angel, that means he is part of God's creation. I always had a problem with this. If God is the author and creator of all there is, He could have written a different script. If He did, then, He would not have had to send His 'so-called Son' to die such a terrible death on the cross in order to fix everything that went wrong. Becky, there is too much suffering in the world for me to believe there is a God who is in control. Where is He when a little child is kidnapped, raped, and murdered? Where is He when a crane falls and kills several people walking below? Where is He when a drunk driver plows into a car and kills or maims innocent people?

"Why are we called sinners? Why is mankind to blame for everything that went wrong? I never did anything really bad and neither did you, Becky. And how does something that supposedly happened thousands of years ago have anything to do with us now? I'm a rational being. I rely on what I can see and understand. I leave the mysteries of life to the philosophers."

Becky, very surprised, said, "Charlie, I never knew you felt this way. It is amazing that we had to travel all this distance to have this conversation. I consider myself a rational person, too, but I believe there is more to life than what I can see, touch, and feel. The unseen or supernatural world is just as real as the seen or natural world. It is mankind's total reality.

"We are finite creatures, limited by our finite senses. God, on the other hand, is not finite. He stands outside His creation and transcends it. That's why when He was here, He could walk on water, heal the blind, and raise the dead. He made the natural laws and can suspend them at will.

"I don't know why He created the world the way He did, but He is God, and I am not. He doesn't owe us an explanation. He didn't have to create anything at all. He is all sufficient and doesn't need anyone. After the fall, He wanted to help us. So He decided—using men as His prophets—to tell us the whole story of creation and reveal who He is. He did this because He loves us. The Bible is our map, compass, and our North Star which will guide us all the way to our real home which is in heaven. It reveals who God is, what happened as the result of the fall, why we are in the predicament we are in, and His loving plan to restore everything that was lost in the garden. His redemptive plan involved the sacrificial death of His only Son, Jesus the Messiah. The Jewish people rejected Him, thinking He was an imposter, but He wasn't. He was and is the real deal. Charlie, we made a big mistake. But the good news is that it is not too late. He is waiting for us to return to Him."

Charlie interrupted. "It's all a fairy tale, Becky."

Becky replied, "No, it's not a fairy tale. There is not

going to be a happy ending for everyone."

"That's another thing," Charlie said. "Only certain people will enter heaven."

"Yes, Charlie, only those who believe."

"See, Becky, He's writing the script."

"No, Charlie, we have free will. We are not characters in a script. We have freedom of choice. We can say 'yes' or 'no.' Oh, Charlie, I can see we are light years apart in how we view life. Do you remember when we were in the school play last year? Do you remember what Hamlet said?"

"What did he say? He said many things," Charlie responded.

Becky answered, "Hamlet said, 'There are more things in heaven and Earth, Horatio, than are dreamt of in your philosophy.'[105] Charlie, we are here in Israel—the land where everything began. I hope you can keep an open mind."

Charlie looked down, staring at his lunch, but said nothing.

After lunch, Charlie walked Becky back to the main office on the base, and they warmly hugged each other

---

105. Shakespeare, William. *Hamlet*, scene 1, Act 5.

and said goodbye.

"Charlie, take good care of yourself. I love you, and you know who loves you more? Jesus!"

"Don't start that with me," said Charlie. "You are barking up the wrong tree. I was born a Jew and will remain a Jew. Unlike you, I am very proud of that."

Though frustrated, Becky didn't say anything. With those last words ringing in her ears, Charlie kissed Becky goodbye and walked away. Becky watched him as he left. A strange feeling came over her. She couldn't identify the feeling, but it was not a good feeling. It was as if he was slowly fading away. She found a bench and sat down to wait for Gloria.

CHAPTER 15

In a little while, Gloria's car arrived. Roger was in the car, too. Becky shared with them her meeting and conversation with Charlie saying, "It was difficult but much better than I expected. At least, we didn't come to blows."

"That's very good. I was praying for you. Now, let's take you on a tour of old Jerusalem. There are a lot of wonderful shops there," said Gloria.

The car arrived in the old city, and Gloria parked on a side street. They spent several hours strolling through the streets of old Jerusalem. "I know a nice café nearby where we can get some good coffee and great dessert." Seated at the café, they ordered coffee and cake. Their conversation naturally drifted toward Jesus.

They were not aware that their conversation was being overheard by a couple at a nearby table. After a while, the man at the table interrupted them and snarled. "I don't want to hear about Jesus. Why don't you take your conversation outside?"

Roger responded, "I'm sorry, but we are having a private conversation."

This only angered the man more, and he said, "Well, we came in here to relax, not to hear you proselytize your meshugana [crazy] belief that Jesus is the Messiah."

"We weren't proselytizing. We were just talking among ourselves. Why don't you just move to another table?" Roger politely replied.

The man looked at his companion and stood up, saying, "Don't tell me what to do." Then, he picked up a basket of sticky buns and threw them at Roger.

Gloria reached up and tried to grab Roger's arm, but she was too late. Roger jumped to his feet, brushed the crumbs off his shirt, and moved toward the man. The man threw a punch at Roger, and one thing led to another.

Becky tried to intervene by explaining that they were Jews too. "We are Jewish-Christians," she exclaimed.

By now, the other people in the café were watching and listening. They were visibly upset and began to shout, "Get out of here. Do you know what you are? Meshumads, that's what you are!" one lady shouted.

Another man stood up and said, "You are really anti-Semites in disguise. We don't want you here! Go back where you came from."

Becky tried to engage the crowd in a conversation and explain what a Jewish-Christian was, but they weren't receptive. In fact, the more she talked, the angrier they were. The tension in the café increased, and the atmosphere became extremely hostile very quickly. People got up from their tables and surrounded Roger, Gloria, and Becky. They tried to exit the café, but the crowd pushed and shoved them, and Roger fell against one of the display counters and broke it.

Soon, the sound of sirens could be heard. Someone in

the café had called the police. The owner of the café told the police that it was all Roger, Gloria, and Becky's fault, and they were arrested. The three of them were charged with disturbing the peace and proselytizing. They spent a night in jail, and the next morning, they were brought before the magistrate.

The Israeli prosecutor began his opening statement. "Your honor, these three people—transplanted Americans—have been arrested for causing a disturbance in Jerusalem and proselytizing. A café owner sustained a lot of damage in his store when a fight broke out."

"What was the reason for the melee?" asked the judge.

"They were telling people that Jesus was the Messiah of Israel," the prosecutor replied.

The judge turned to Roger, Gloria, and Becky. "Oh, I see. Well," addressing all three, "what do you have to say?"

Becky stepped forward. "Your honor, we didn't mean to cause a disturbance. We were just having something to eat and talking among ourselves. A couple at a nearby table heard us talking about Jesus because we are Jewish-

Christians, and they got very upset. Quite frankly, I don't understand why the people got so mad. We weren't bothering anyone."

The judge gave her a half smile. "You sound very naïve, young lady. The name of Jesus and Jews are like water and oil. They don't mix well. Anyway, I want to hear what you told them."

"I tried to explain what a Jewish-Christian means, but they wouldn't listen. A few of them started shouting at us saying there is no such thing. 'Either you are a Jew or a Christian, you can't be both,' they said. And they were yelling at us, 'Meshumad, meshumad.' I asked someone what that meant. It means, traitor. Your honor, we are not traitors. Please let me try and explain.

"We are simply Jewish people who have accepted Jesus as the long-promised Messiah of Israel. Most of Jesus's followers in the beginning were Jewish people. Jesus, Himself, was Jewish. Those who accepted Jesus as the Messiah were called Jewish-Christians. That means followers of Christ, the anointed One or the Messiah.

Those who did not accept Jesus as the Messiah retained their original identity as Jewish and clung to the Older Testament Scriptures. They did not understand that the Jewish Scriptures spoke often of a coming Messiah and described in detail how to identify Him when He came.

"It was the many prophecies and the miracles which Jesus performed which pointed to Him as being the fulfillment of the prophecies. They were His credentials. And by the way, I pointed out to them that Jesus was sent by the God of Abraham, Isaac, and Jacob. He was His Son. When I told them that, they only got angrier."

"Well, I can understand why they were very angry." The judge raised his eyebrows.

The judge looked perplexed as he tried very hard to understand what Becky was saying. He asked her, "Young lady, why do you need to be considered a Jew when most of the Jewish community and probably other people as well consider someone like you a Christian?"

"Your Honor, you are Jewish, aren't you?"

"Yes, I am," the judge responded.

"Would you give up being Jewish for any reason?"

"No," said the judge firmly. "I never would, under any condition. I was born a Jew, and I will die a Jew."

"Well, your honor, I will never give up being Jewish either. While I am proud to be a Christian now, it is very important to me that I also retain my Jewish identity. I was born Jewish, just like you and just like Jesus. He, too, was born a Jew, and He died a Jew. He told a woman He met at a well in Samaria that He was the Messiah of Israel. I believe He was speaking the truth." Becky paused and thought for a moment and then said, "You know, your honor, I just realized something. All of Christianity crumbles if Jesus isn't the Messiah of Israel. It is based on that belief."

The judge looked at Becky for a long time and finally said, "I think it is time we take a recess. I will be back in two hours with my verdict."

When the courtroom session reconvened, the judge entered, sat down, and asked Becky, Gloria, and Roger to rise.

He said, "I am ready to render my verdict in this

case." Looking at Becky, he said, "Young lady, I believe you are very sincere in your belief. However, you and your friends were responsible for causing a public disturbance. As a result, damage to private property was sustained. I am ordering the three of you to pay the owner of the cafe for those damages. Because this is your first offense, I am cautioning you to avoid causing another disturbance. I don't want to see any of you in my courtroom again. You are dismissed."

CHAPTER 16

Several months passed. Becky became involved in her studies at the university. She made some friends and dated a few very nice young men. Because they were Jewish, she was very careful about discussing her faith in Jesus. Her recent experience in the café, subsequent arrest, and court appearance had taught her a painful lesson.

She was quite comfortable living with Gloria and Roger and postponed her search for her own apartment. They went to church on Sundays, and during the week, she attended the university. Her plan to get acquainted with life in Israel seemed to be working. However, she did wonder why she hadn't had a visit from Jesus recently.

Then, one night, everything changed very dramatically. The ring of the telephone tore into the stillness of the night. It was 2:00 a.m. The call was for Becky. She ran down the stairs saying to Gloria who had picked up the phone, "Who could be calling me at this hour?"

It was the captain of Charlie's air force base. He asked Becky to come to the base immediately. She tried to get some information, but he only would say, "Please come quickly."

Becky, Gloria, and Roger dressed, got into the car, and sped to the base. Upon arrival at the main office, they were met with the somber-looking captain. He had a very grim look on his face and said, "Who is Becky?" Becky slowly raised her hand; her heart began to beat very fast. "I have very bad news for you," he said. "Your brother, Charlie, was killed in a training exercise earlier this evening. We did everything we could to revive him, but it was no use. I am so sorry. He was a wonderful young man."

Becky gasped and reached out her arm to Gloria to steady herself. The room began to spin, and she thought, *I'm going to faint.* Gloria and Roger immediately put their arms around Becky and walked to the nearby lounge to sit down.

The captain followed them and said, "It was a routine flight, but something catastrophic happened, and Charlie lost control of the plane, and it crashed. We had no radio contact, and we can't find the black box."

Becky looked at him, trying to comprehend what he was saying, but she couldn't. *Routine flight, catastrophic, lost control, black box, words, just words. What do they mean?* she thought. She looked at her watch. "It's 3:00 a.m. What are we doing here? Am I dreaming?" She was clearly in shock.

After several hours, the three of them returned to their apartment. Becky just stared at the ceiling in her room and cried, "This is all my fault." Suddenly, she jumped up, exclaiming out loud, "Oh, I have to call my mother and grandmother." She looked at the clock and thought, *I'll call a little later.*

Totally exhausted, physically and emotionally, Becky took a sleeping pill, lay down on the bed, and fell into a very deep sleep. When she awoke, she looked at the clock again. It was now 1:00 p.m. (6:00 a.m. in New York). The events of the previous night came flooding back. *Maybe I had a nightmare and dreamt it all*, Becky thought.

She quickly showered, dressed, and went downstairs. Roger and Gloria were seated at the table having a late breakfast. From the look on their faces, Becky knew that last night was not a dream. "Why don't you sit with us and have some breakfast, and then, we'll map out a plan," Gloria said.

"I have to call my mother, have Charlie's body sent home, and make arrangements for my own trip home," Becky replied.

"Roger and I will do all we can to help you," Gloria said.

Thanking them, Becky finished eating what little she could swallow. "Can I use your phone? I'll reimburse you for the charges."

"Of course, use the phone in the den. You'll have more privacy there, and don't worry about the phone charges," responded Roger.

Becky got up from the table, walked into the den, and closed the door. She picked up the phone and gave the operator her home number in Brooklyn. A few minutes passed, and Becky heard the phone ring. She held her breath. The familiar voice on the other end said, "Hello." It was Becky's mother.

"Hi, Mom. How are you?"

Surprised to hear Becky's voice so early in the morning, her mother said, "Is everything okay?"

Becky replied, "Is Grandma around?"

"Yes, she is. Why?" her mother anxiously responded.

"Can you please ask her to come to the phone." Becky urged. There was a pause, and she could hear her mother calling her grandmother.

"What's wrong? Something is wrong. I can hear it in your voice," Becky's mother said.

"I have terrible news. Charlie is dead. He was killed

last night in a training exercise."

Becky heard her mother gasp and her grandmother cry out, "Gestorben? Oy vey, Charlie gestorben [death]? What happened?"

Becky explained the circumstances, and Becky heard her mother's voice again. She was crying and yelled, "It's all your fault. If you hadn't started this Jesus business, Charlie wouldn't have gone to Israel to redefine his identity as a Jew."

Becky gripped the phone tightly in her hand as if to lean on it for support. She was reeling and took several deep breaths. She tried to calm her mother down, but that was almost impossible to do on the phone. "I'll call you again in a few hours with more information," she managed to blurt out in confusion and fear.

Becky hung up the phone, sat down in the nearest chair, and began to sob. Her crying was loud and uncontrollable. Gloria opened the door, rushed in, and asked, "What happened?"

Becky, breathlessly told her, and then said, "What am

I going to do? She blames me."

"That's not fair. Charlie made a choice to come here. He didn't have to. Your mother is lashing out in her grief and pain," Gloria said.

"I'd better keep busy, or I'm going to go crazy. I told the base captain I would call him," Becky replied. Gloria picked up the phone, called the air force base, asked for the captain, and handed the phone to Becky. After a short pause, he was on the phone.

"Hello, Becky, I was waiting for your call. How are you?"

Becky's voice was shaky. "I've been better, of course. I'm just calling to make the final arrangements."

The captain and Becky talked for a little while and discussed plans for Charlie's body to be sent home. He told Becky that he had made it possible for Becky to accompany Charlie's body on the plane. Becky thanked him and hung up. Gloria said, "Let's go to church. I think we need to pray." Becky nodded her head in agreement.

Becky, Gloria, and Roger walked slowly through the

streets and entered the sanctuary of the church. It was a weekday afternoon, so the church was almost empty.

A young couple were up front, praying. They remained in the church for some time in silent meditation. The stillness and the biblical pictures on the wall helped Becky refocus. Then, they took a slow walk through the streets, found a café nearby, and ordered some coffee. Becky thanked Gloria and Roger for their support. She was feeling very fragile.

After they returned to the apartment, Becky found the courage and strength to call her mother again. She gave her the final details about the arrival of Charlie's body and told her that she would be accompanying his casket. Quite to Becky's shock and horror, her mother said, "I don't want you to come home. Your presence at the funeral will only upset everyone. I don't know what happened to you. Once, we were very close, but right now, you are a stranger to me. Go, follow your Jesus. I hope He doesn't disappoint you as you have disappointed me." Becky's mother cried and hung up the phone.

Becky, crying now too, turned to Gloria saying, "What shall I do? My mother doesn't want me to come home and attend Charlie's funeral. She said if I were there, everyone would be upset. I feel like I am having a nightmare."

Gloria put her arm around Becky's shoulder saying, "I think you have to honor your mother's wishes. She's right. Your family will be upset. They don't understand, and you won't be able to help them understand."

Becky and Gloria prayed together, and Becky decided to follow Gloria's advice. She called the captain at the air force base and told him that her family situation was very complicated, and she would not be able to accompany Charlie's body home. The captain said that he would take care of everything.

Feeling exhausted, Becky slowly climbed the stairs to her room and sat in a lounge chair. She almost dozed off when the circle of colors appeared in the center of the room.

The familiar, gentle voice greeted Becky. "Hello, Becky, I'm so sorry about Charlie. I know how much you and Charlie loved each other in spite of your differences."

Becky didn't look up. "I feel terrible. It's all my fault. He wouldn't have died if I hadn't become a Christian missionary. He was struggling with his Jewish identity because of me. That's why he came to Israel and joined the Israeli Air Force."

"I know you are heartbroken, but don't blame yourself. Charlie's time was up. Man's days are numbered. I numbered them before time began. I promised you that I would be with you in the good times and the bad times. I'm here to comfort you now. Lean on Me. Let Me help you get through this. You can share your deepest feelings with Me. I am not only your Lord and Savior; I am your friend."[106]

Becky rose to her feet. "You want me to tell You how I honestly feel?" She was very angry and raised her voice. "Okay, I'll tell You how I feel! I feel like I'm being punished because I chose to follow You. Before I met You, everything in my life was moving along nicely. Not perfectly, but normally. I had minor problems here and there, but nothing major. And I had a family. After You appeared, everything

---

106. Psalms 139:16.

changed. Basically, I lost my family. Everyone turned on me. Now, here I am, thousands of miles from home. My father is dead, Charlie is gone, and my grandmother thinks I am a Nazi! And to top it off, my mother, whom I just talked to on the telephone this morning, told me not to come home because she blames me for Charlie's death. I'm sorry, but You asked me to share my feelings with You."[107]

"Becky, when I asked you to follow Me, I didn't promise you that it would be an easy road or that you would understand everything that happened on your journey. However, I did promise I would be with you, and here I am.[108]

"From the very beginning, I knew all about you and how our relationship would impact you and your family. I also knew that you are someone who keeps the commitments they make, no matter what happens. Charlie would have died when he did even if we hadn't met, so it is not your fault. There are things about life I can't explain to you. Now, you see only in part. Someday, you will see the

107. Psalms 73:13–14.
108. John 16:33.

whole picture, and you will have a very different perspective. On that day, when you stand on heaven's shores, you will see everything more clearly.[109]

"You won't have any questions then, as hard as that is to believe now. You need to trust Me and know that through it all, I am leading you to My kingdom which is not of this world. Because you belong to Me, My Holy Spirit lives within you, and you will have all the strength you need to overcome this tragedy.

"If in your human nature you sometimes feel overwhelmed, that's normal. I will carry you." He paused. "You are angry at Me, aren't you?"

"Yes," said Becky. "Well, You asked me to share my feelings with You. Now, I feel guilty for being mad at You. I know You are God, and I am not! I'm sorry, I shouldn't have raised my voice."

"Your anger is rooted in fear. You have been dealing with a lot. I will pray for you that your faith will not fail. Remember who I am, why I came into this world, and that

---

109. 1 Corinthians 13:9–13.

we have an adversary.[110]

"He will try to convince you that you made a mistake when you accepted Me and that you should give up. That is a lie. I have given you everything you need to persevere and endure to the end. In fact, the Scriptures say, as a follower of Mine, you are blessed in the heavenly realms with every spiritual blessing in Me [Ephesians 1:3, NIV].

"Keep this in mind. When I carried the heavy cross, I stumbled and fell under its weight. I was weak, in terrible pain from the beatings I endured, and I was hungry and thirsty. But I didn't give up. Do you know what kept Me going? Not only was it love for My Father who had sent Me here, it was knowing how much was hanging in the balance and dependent upon My climbing all the way to the top of the hill. My Father had given Me a charge to keep. My purpose was to save souls.[111]

"I was sent here with the power and words of eternal life. Everyone who believed Me at that time and all who followed after them—and that includes you—would

---

110. Luke 22:31–32.
111. Hebrews 12:2.

be forgiven of their sins and live forever in heaven. *'Sins forgiven, and heaven gained. Sins forgiven, and heaven gained. Sins forgiven, and heaven gained'* was what I kept thinking as I took each agonizing step on that dusty road. When I finally reached the top of the hill and was being nailed to the cross, I could have called ten thousand angels to come and rescue Me, but I didn't. I finished the work My Father gave Me to do.[112]

"Now, the question for you, Becky, is, can you carry your cross? Every disciple of Mine will have to carry a cross. But always remember, I will carry the heavier end of it because you are fulfilling My will for your life. Can you think of anything more meaningful and fulfilling than being the instrument that helps someone obtain forgiveness and eternal life?[113]

"One day, Becky, you will write the story about your encounter with Me. Because you are a Jew, you will write it from a Jewish perspective. But I love everyone. I died for everyone. However, I do have a special place in My

112. Matthew 26:53.
113. Luke 9:23.

heart for the Jewish people. That's where My story as the incarnated son of man began. It began with them.

"As their Messiah, I identify with them and all of their persecutions and sufferings. Their sufferings and Mine were the result of sinful, corrupted hearts. The difference is that I was able to do something about men and women's sin nature. On the cross, not only was I crucified, but their sin nature was crucified as well. And as a result, every man and woman has a second chance to have a relationship with Me. The first opportunity was forfeited in the garden."

"You say You are the Jews' Messiah, but the Holocaust still happened, and I still don't have an adequate answer to their question. 'Why did a loving God allow it?' Telling them that it is the result of the fall of man doesn't mean anything to some of them. Some of them don't believe in the Bible, and some don't even believe there is a God!"

Jesus replied, "Every manner of suffering and death has existed since Adam and Eve were expelled from the garden. The Holocaust was one very brutal and ugly chapter of man's inhumanity to man. There have been many others. None of those evil events were part of My original design. As I told you, I designed everything there is and called it "good." When Adam disobeyed Me, he, in essence, tossed My script away and wrote his own. Since he was the representative head of the human race, what he did affected everyone who was born after him. It is Adam's legacy. The sinful acts of man, the unthinkable tragedies, and the deep, deep sorrows of life are all part of the script that man wrote. I wouldn't have written such a story."

Becky interrupted. "I don't understand. No one would want any of those terrible things to happen, and who would write a script like that?"

"It's the consequences of choices, Becky," Jesus replied. He continued, "Do you remember your pastor saying, 'You can choose your sin, but you can't choose the consequences?'"

"Yes, I do."

"The script that man wrote is the consequence of sinful choices unfolding, Becky. Unknowingly, when Adam disobeyed Me, he stepped into a cosmic battle between

Myself and the devil, and he became the devil's pawn. That's the risk I took when I gave men free will. But I have always been in charge of everything, and I stand outside of My creation—sovereign and in control.

"That's why, at a certain moment in time, I thrust a cross into the ground. It was the dividing line between the old order of things and the new. It was there that man's sin debt was paid, it was there I conquered death, and it was there that man was given a second chance. It's another chance to live out the original script that I wrote. Only I can redeem the past.

"Not to trivialize or diminish the pain that usually accompanies the question of pain and suffering, perhaps you can introduce this question into the conversation. 'Why did an innocent man suffer and die on the cross for the sins of the whole world?'"

"I don't know if answering a question with another question is going to help, but I'll try. Also, there is an additional problem. Some people are saying that the Holocaust never happened."

"Becky, if someone tells you that, don't argue with them. Just walk away. That person believes a lie. He or she has been deceived by the master deceiver, Satan. I knew that, one day, people would deny the fact that the Holocaust happened, and that lie would be a sword that would pierce many hearts. But the truth always prevails.

"And one of the truths that has prevailed is the survival of the Jewish people, against all odds, because of a promise that I made to them many, many years ago. I told them, through My prophet Jeremiah, 'Behold, the days are coming, declares the Lord, when I will make a new covenant with the house of Israel... Thus, says the Lord, who gives the sun for light by day and the fixed order of the moon and the stars for light by night. If this fixed order departs from before Me, declares the Lord, then shall the offspring of Israel cease from being a nation before Me forever' [Jeremiah 31:31–36, NIV]. That means that the light from the sun, moon, and stars would have to be extinguished before Israel would cease to exist.

"I kept My promise, Becky. I didn't promise them that

they wouldn't have to go through much tribulation, but I did promise them that they would survive. And they did, and they always will. I am the Messiah of Israel. I have placed My name in Jerusalem, My Holy City. It belongs to Me. And no weapon formed against Israel will prevail. I am not saying weapons won't be formed, but they will never prevail!"

Becky responded by saying, "You know, there is another problem I don't have a handle on. The old question of heaven and hell. A lot of people don't believe there is a heaven or a hell, and if they do and I mention hell, they say I am unloving. What shall I tell them?"

"Give them this illustration, Becky. Suppose someone is travelling at night on a country road in a storm. Further down the road, there is an old wooden bridge located over a deep river, but it has been destroyed by the storm. Now, the road leads down a steep embankment into the river. Suddenly, a man appears on the side of the road with a lantern and flags the car down. He tells the driver that he has received word that the bridge has been washed out. Is that a loving or unloving thing to do? Doesn't that man's action typify the true meaning of love, caring for another. The stranger on the road didn't have to go out into the storm to give the warning. He could have stayed in his warm, dry house and said nothing."

Becky remarked, "So there really is a heaven and a hell?"

"Yes, Becky, and the choice where someone spends eternity is up to him or her. My heart aches every time someone makes the wrong choice."

"And no one goes to heaven without being covered by Your blood. It doesn't have anything to do with how good or bad they are. Is that right?"

"Yes, Becky, that's the way I designed the way back to Me. If people accept Me as their Savior, they enter heaven wearing My robe of righteousness which covers all of their sins. It's not someone's own righteousness that gains them entrance to heaven but only Mine! Mankind does not have any righteousness of their own."

"People don't like to hear that," replied Becky,

'Be brave, Becky. Don't think of quitting now just

because things are tough. Think of the prize—the souls of men and women who will read your story and be saved."

Becky was only half listening. She was lost in her own thoughts and asked, "Where is Charlie now? Will I see him again? He didn't accept you as his Messiah."

"Becky, as difficult as this is for you, I have to tell you the truth. Charlie had many opportunities to hear the Gospel message. You spoke of Me often. Unfortunately, he made a choice, not knowing that his time would soon run out. Many people act as if they will live forever, forgetting that My Word says that their days are numbered.[114]

"Sadly, like Charlie, they miss the 'God moments' when I break through the routine of their daily living. Either they don't recognize them, or they simply dismiss them. 'God moments' can occur anytime and anywhere. I can speak through a loved one, a friend, or a stranger. I can touch a heart through an inspirational song or through words in a book. But My gentle, still voice can be heard most clearly in the quiet times which are set aside to meditate on My Word—the Bible.

114. Psalms 139:16.

"There are people who live their whole lives as if I were irrelevant. They don't give much thought to Me at all. Their focus is on worldly things which will pass away. They acquire a lot of material things and live quite comfortably for a while, but it is only for a season. And the season, all too soon, comes to an end. Only three things will last forever—Myself, My Word [the Bible], and My people [all those who believe in Me].

"The Bible is a map and a compass which I gave to mankind so that they can successfully navigate through their life's journey. But Satan and the powers of darkness blind their eyes and hide the truth from them. However, I have many believers throughout the world. My followers punch holes in the darkness and dispel the lies with the light of My truth."[115]

Becky seemed totally lost in her own thoughts and asked, "What did Charlie lose?"

Jesus paused for a moment, and in a voice filled with compassion, said, "Everything that really matters... Everything that has eternal value."

115. 2 Corinthians 4:4–6.

Becky looked at Jesus's face and saw that His eyes were filled with tears. He said, "I am so sorry, Becky. That is why it is important to share the Gospel story. I am this world's only hope."

Becky was crying and said, "Charlie was so young, and he was really a good person. We fought a lot like siblings do, but we had a strong bond between us. When we were at school, he used to protect me from bullies. This seems so unfair."

"There is a lot I can't explain to you now, but try to remember that death is the result of the fall of man. Remember, too, that I died to overrule the works of Satan. Salvation doesn't have anything to do with someone being good or bad. It is not based on your performance. It is based on something that I did on the cross. It is all of grace. It is a gift. But for a gift to be of value to the one to whom it is offered, it must be accepted. On the cross, I reset the clock, and mankind is offered another chance. I am making all things new. A day is coming when there will be no more death, no sorrow, no more sickness, no more goodbyes. I will wipe away the tears from your eyes forever."[116]

"I believe You, but I can't think about what Charlie lost. I don't know if I can bear to hear this. I shouldn't have asked." Tears were flowing down her cheeks.

"I knew you would ask. Your mission to the Jewish people will always have a sorrowful shadow across its path—the memory of Charlie. It will be your cross. But that memory will fill you with a sense of urgency about sharing the Gospel message. As you speak to people, you will always remember the wrong choice he made, and as painful as it will be, it will deepen your witness. You will speak from your heart, not your head, and the Gospel message will be heard, like music, in a major not a minor chord."[117]

Becky was sobbing. "I don't think I can do this. I know I'm being selfish, but how am I going to witness to people and watch some of them accept You, knowing that Charlie won't be in heaven?"

116. Revelation 7:1, 21:4.
117. Romans 9:1–5.

"Becky, remember this. Who comes into My kingdom and who does not is not under your control. You have been given the privilege of being one of My instruments, one of many that I have. You and they plant the seeds. I water and give the increase. I'm the one who saves. Becky, you need to lean on Me now. Please remember that I love you." Something in His gentle voice began to heal her pain. She felt a deep sense of peace.

With these words, the swirl of colors slowly faded, and Jesus was gone.

Chapter 17

The following months were challenging for Becky. She often thought of her mother and grandmother, whom she loved, but accepted her present situation as God's will for her. That gave her some peace of mind. However, whenever she thought of Charlie, her heart ached.

She went to church often, became involved with some church programs, and shared her faith wherever and whenever possible. Her schoolwork kept her very busy. She studied Hebrew, the history of Israel, and became more familiar with the land by taking special bus tours. Becky loved Israel and began to feel that it was her real home.

She had been in Israel for almost a year when she received a phone call from one of her cousins saying that her mother was very ill with cancer and that she should come home. Her cousin told Becky that her mother was asking for her. It was during the Chanukah/Christmas break, so Becky immediately booked a plane for New York. The captain at Charlie's air force base helped her get a flight home.

When the plane landed at JFK, she disembarked and took a cab straight to her house. Her grandmother opened the door saying, through her tears, "Becky, you are here." Becky and her grandmother hugged each other. "Your mother is upstairs. She is very ill, and a nurse is with her," her grandmother said.

Becky dropped her bags in the vestibule and went immediately upstairs. When she entered her mother's dimly-lit room, she saw her mother was sitting in a chair. The nurse was straightening the bed. When her mother saw Becky, she said, "Oh, Becky, my baby, you came. I am so sorry for all the things I said to you. You know I love you."

"It's okay, Mom. I understand." Becky approached her mother and hugged and kissed her.

Sensing that Becky and her mother wanted to be alone, the nurse excused herself and left the room.

Becky fed her mother some soup, adjusted the pillow in her chair, combed her hair, and then, sat down on the floor at her mother's feet and said, "Mom, you know I love you very much. I wouldn't lead you astray. I don't fully understand why Jesus appeared to me, but I do know who He is, and I know He will help you and be with you for the rest of your journey."

She didn't want to mention the word "death." "Will you pray with me?" Quite to Becky's surprise, her mother shook her head "yes."

Now, what am I going to do? she thought. *My Bible is downstairs. I don't want to leave her for a moment and miss this opportunity.* She prayed silently for Jesus's help. As she was quietly praying, Becky felt an indescribable presence in the room. It covered her like a blanket of peace. She knew it was Jesus. He wasn't visible, but He was very, very close.

Her eyes filled with tears, and she gently took her mother's hands saying, "Mom, just listen to what I am saying, and if you are willing, please repeat after me. Oh, God, I don't understand what has happened to Becky. But something very unusual did happen. I can tell. She told me that Jesus is the Mashiach. If He is the promised Messiah, I don't want to make a mistake and reject Him. Please forgive me for all of my sins and open my heart so I can receive Him as my Mashiach. I accept Him by faith. Becky said if I sincerely reach out to You, You will help me. God, I need Your help."

Becky's mother repeated what Becky said, one sentence at a time. Becky took one of her mother's hands saying, "Mom, now I am going to place your hand in the hand of Jesus by faith. If this is okay, just nod your head 'yes.'"

Her mother nodded her head in agreement. Becky took a deep breath and bowed her head. "Thank You, Jesus. Now, she belongs to You." Becky cried softly.

CHAPTER 18

Becky spent the next few days enjoying quality time with her mother and grandmother. Tensions between them had subsided. She told them about life in Israel, omitting the religious part. She felt welcomed and was glad to be home.

Neither Becky nor her mother told her grandmother what had transpired in her mother's room.

Becky made plans to spend Christmas Eve with her friend, Barbara. She went to bed early because she felt some jet lag. At 3:00 a.m., she was awakened by the sound of voices in the hallway. She jumped out of bed, put on her robe, opened her bedroom door, and peered out.

Two medical attendants were in the hallway. They were carrying her mother down the stairs to a waiting ambulance. Her grandmother stood at the top of the stairs crying. "She's very sick. I think she is going to die."

Becky quickly dressed, and she and her grandmother took a taxi to the hospital. When they arrived, her mother had already been admitted to the emergency room. Becky and her grandmother waited in the hospital lounge. Several hours later, a doctor approached them and said, "I'm sorry but she is experiencing heart failure. Prepare yourselves."

They remained at the hospital all day and were able to spend some time with Becky's mother as she slipped in and out of consciousness. Becky cancelled her Christmas Eve dinner with Barbara and returned to the hospital lounge.

At around 4:30 p.m. one of the attending physicians approached them saying, "I'm sorry, but she just passed away while she was sleeping."

Becky jumped up from her seat and blurted out, "She can't die on Christmas Eve!" The doctor and her grandmother were startled. "I don't know why I said that," Becky exclaimed.

Becky and her grandmother made the necessary arrangements at the hospital and returned home. It was now around 9:00 p.m. Becky hugged and kissed her grandmother good night and went to her room. She had been up since 3:00 a.m. the night before.

As she was preparing for bed, Becky suddenly was filled with joy. The feeling was so intense that she wanted to go on the rooftop and dance! She couldn't understand what was happening. *I must be having a breakdown. This is not normal,* she thought.

Concerned, she called one of the elders at the church. She told him what she was experiencing, and he said, "Becky, I know what is happening. There is no way, humanly speaking, that you could experience such joy tonight right after your mother just died. I know how much you loved your mother. God's Holy Spirit is telling you that your mother is with Him tonight! What a Christmas gift He is giving you! Don't try and analyze it. Just receive it."

They prayed for a little while, and then, Becky sat by her bedroom window looking up at the stars. "It's Christmas Eve. My mother entered heaven on Christmas Eve! Only You could have arranged for that to happen, Jesus. Thank You. I believe my father is there too, and they are together now," she said out loud. Becky was now weeping tears of joy.

Becky and her family attended her mother's funeral and sat shiva (a time of mourning) for seven days. Becky had to be very careful not to show the joy she was experiencing in her heart; otherwise, her family would think she was in denial.

Her buoyant spirit only lasted for a week, and then, she began to deeply mourn the loss of her mother.

She and her grandmother spent several weeks together, but they never spoke about Jesus. There was an unspoken truce between them. They decided to sell the family house, and Becky's grandmother moved into a close friend's home. She didn't want to remain alone in the house with all of its memories.

Becky returned to Israel and resumed her new life

there. She caught up with her studies at the university and was very happy to be back with Gloria, Roger, and her friends at church.

One evening, soon after she returned to Israel, as she was preparing to go to bed, Jesus appeared to her. She hadn't seen Him since her mother died. In a gentle tone He said, "Hello, Becky."

Becky replied, "I'm so happy to see You. I have been waiting to thank You for saving my mother. I felt Your presence in the room that day. You were very, very close."

"Yes, I was there. She is with Me now. Your father is, too," Jesus said.

Becky looked at Him and smiled. "Now, we have to get Grandma on board. That's going to be much harder."

Jesus smiled, "I know your grandmother better than you do. Her heart is not as hard as you think. Why don't you get some rest now? You need to focus on your schoolwork and your church activities.[118] I will come back soon and share my future plans for you. As you drift off into sleep tonight, meditate on My love for you. That will

118. Psalms 139:1–4.

help you overcome some of your recent experiences. Always remember, no matter what happens, I will never leave you or forsake you."[119]

"I love You too," replied Becky.

---

119. Psalms 1:1–3; Matthew 28:20.

CHAPTER 19

Becky's grandmother sat in the living room thinking about what had happened during the last year. First her son-in-law died of cancer, then, her only child and daughter died of cancer as well. Her grandson joined the Israeli Air Force and was killed, and her granddaughter, whom she loved so much, is in Israel, running around and telling everyone she meets that Jesus is the Mashiach. She cried softly.

Suddenly, the room was filled with the swirl of many colors. Jesus was in the midst of the circle and began to talk to her.

"Don't be afraid," He said. "I am Jesus, and I have

come to talk to you."

Startled, she raised her arm up, shielding her face saying, "Stay away, don't come near me. You are not real."

"I am real. You don't have to be afraid. I know you are going through a very difficult time."

She wiped away some tears and said, "Well, I don't understand what is happening. Maybe this whole thing is just a bad dream, and I will wake up soon. I feel my world has turned upside down. It reminds me of the time when I was a little girl. Everything changed so quickly then, and it was all terrible. I saw and heard things that no one should have seen and heard."

"I did too," said Jesus. "And what I have seen and heard for thousands of years has been worse. Mankind can be very mean-spirited and cruel."[120]

"My family and I were chased out of our homeland because we were hated."

"I was, too. I was beaten, spat upon, and forced to carry a heavy cross outside of Jerusalem, a place I considered

---

120. Jeremiah 17:9.

My home."[121]

"We had to leave a lot of our relatives, our friends, our house, our clothes, and our wonderful dog, Sparky. My parents were afraid that his barking would draw attention to us, so we gave him to one of our neighbors. I still remember his big brown eyes and bewildered look as we closed the door and left him behind." She was weeping now.

"I, too, had to leave behind My relatives and friends, and the Romans took My garments from Me. I understand how you feel."[122]

"You do? And You are really Jesus?" She was more composed now. She wiped away some tears.

He smiled gently. "Yes, I do understand. It was for those tears I died. During your life's journey, eventually, you will have to let go of everything. However, there is one thing you can never lose and that is a relationship with Me. I will be with you always. I promise never to leave or forsake you. I love you."

"How can You be the Mashiach? You are the 'other one.'"

---

121. Isaiah 53:1–12.
122. Matthew 26:47–48, 27:35.

"No, I am not the 'other one.' I am the One the Jewish people have been waiting for."[123]

"How can that be? How did we miss that?"

"It doesn't matter. I am here now. Will you accept Me now? Will you take My hand and let Me lead you to your new home?"

She thought for several minutes then said, "To be honest, taking Your hand is going to be very hard for me. I keep seeing flashes of the holocaust before my eyes. If You really are the Mashiach, where were You when our people were being killed and thrown into open graves or stuffed into ovens?"[124]

"I saw and heard more than you did, and I wept more than you did. It was for those sins I died."

"And I lost my wonderful dear grandparents." She winced at the memories. "They weren't able to escape in time and died in a concentration camp." Her eyes filled with tears again. "It's so hard to forgive and forget."

Jesus nodded sympathetically. "I know. I, too, had

---

123. John 1:11.
124. Psalms 10:1; 13:1, 14:1–3; 2 Peter 3:4.

to forgive. I was put to death in the most unimaginable cruel way. My Spirit will enable you to forgive, just as I forgave."[125]

Jesus showed her both His hands. "Do you see the holes in My wrists? They are from the nails which held Me to the cross. Now, look at My hands. Tell me what you see."

"I see names written on Your palms."

"Yes, those names are engraved there. If you will accept Me as your Mashiach, I will write your name there as well. And I will lead you to a place where all of your tears will be wiped away. There will be no more sickness, no more sorrow, no more pain."[126]

"Have You come to tell me that I am going to die now?"

He raises one hand and beckons to her. "Don't be afraid. For My followers, death is just a shadow. I overcame death on the cross, so if you take My hand, I will walk with you right through the dark tunnel to the other side. Because of Me and My love for you, you will not die but live."

She flinched. "Oh, I don't know. How can You be

---

125. Luke 23:34.
126. Isaiah 49:16.

the Mashiach?"

"But I am," Jesus gently replied.

"Becky told me You were a Rabbi."

"Yes, that's true."

She thought this over for a while and said, "A Jewish Rabbi, imagine that! I didn't know that. You know, I must confess that I never liked You."

"You never really knew Me, did you?"

"What about the inquisitions and the crusades? Terrible things were done to the Jews during those times by Christians."

"I was misrepresented by people who never knew Me. The real Christian does things not only in My name but in My nature. And My intrinsic nature is love."[127]

"Becky also told me that when You were dying on the cross, You said, 'Father, forgive them, for they don't know what they are doing.'[128] How were You able to do that?"

"They *didn't* know what they were doing. They didn't know who I was, who sent Me, and the gift I was bringing.

127. Romans 2:24; Isaiah 52:5–6.
128. Luke 23:34, NIV.

This lack of understanding continues right up until today. The kind of love I have in My heart is not like human love—limited and finite. It is divine love—unconditional and without limits."[129]

"I was so sure that You were an imposter. Obviously, I was wrong. This is so unexpected. Tell me, what should I do now?"

In a tone both gentle and urging, Jesus said, "Just reach out your hand to Me, by faith, and I will do the rest."

She hesitated for a minute or two, and then, she reached out her hand to Him. Jesus gently took her hand, and she entered the colorful swirl with Him, and they both disappeared.[130]

Jesus and Grandma now stood on heaven's shores. Her eyes opened wide as she took in what was before her.

"This is what your eyes were meant to see. Do you hear the music? That's what your ears were meant to hear. And you will see and hear this for all of eternity, and you will forget the other things. I prepared all of this for you

---

129. Jeremiah 31:3.
130. John 14:1–3.

and all of My believers."

She smiled and looked into His face. "I do hear the beautiful music, and it fills my whole being. It's as if a full symphony is playing inside of me."

Jesus returned her smile. "It's the heavenly choir rejoicing around the throne. Come walk with Me. Let Me introduce you to My Father."

The Bible reveals that out of the vast ocean of humanity, God chose a small group of people—the Jews—and set them apart with a special purpose in mind. They were to be His holy people, the guardian of His revelation, the keeper of His law, and the means through which the Messiah—the Savior of the world—would come. As the Jewish prophet Isaiah wrote, "I will put salvation in Zion, for Israel My glory" (Isaiah 46:13, NIV).

God told the Jews that He was the only true and living God, and there was no other.[131] He gave them the Holy Scriptures as a sacred trust and called them to reveal Him

131. Isaiah 45:5.

to a mostly pagan world which worshipped many Gods (all of them false). Selecting the Jewish people for this mission was God's sovereign choice.

More than any other group of people, the Jews had privileges and advantages no others had. Chosen by a Holy God, given an amazing revelation of who He is, offered a covenant relationship with Himself (through Abraham, Isaac, Jacob, Moses, and David), entrusted with the law and instructions of the sacrificial system, first in the tabernacle in the wilderness and then the temple, and finally, the promise of a coming Messiah—a Jew, the Son of God— who would be Savior of the world. All this was theirs, a sacred gift from a loving God who is the creator of all there is. They were God's people in a pagan, idolatrous world. He initiated the relationship and fully invested Himself in it. The beginning of their relationship with God couldn't have been better. In today's parlance, "it was theirs to lose."

God's purpose in calling the Jewish people was to display His glory, not only to them but to the whole world. In order for them to do that, He needed a grateful and obedient people. But sadly, as I carefully read the Older Testament Scriptures, I saw very clearly and with much surprise that disobedience and rebellion often marked their relationship with Him. There are many examples of this, but I will choose only one which will illustrate my point. It is well known. It is written in Exodus, the second book of the Torah.

After God had delivered Israel from Egyptian slavery by performing a series of spectacular miracles, including the parting of the Red Sea, the Israelites settled at the base of Mt. Sinai. God called Moses to the top of the mountain to speak to him. A great cloud covered the top of the mountain for all to see. It was the Shekinah glory of God. There, He gave Moses the Ten Commandments and instructions for building the tabernacle. The tabernacle revealed God's heart. He always wanted to dwell with His people as He once did in the garden, but sin now barred the way.

The intricate design of the tabernacle and the sacrificial system opened the way for a holy God to relate to a sinful people (mankind).

Moses had been on the mountain for forty days when the people became impatient saying, "Where is this Moses?" they exclaimed. In his absence, they began to murmur amongst themselves and approached Aaron, Moses's brother, and asked him to create a substitute God for them. They wanted something they could see and touch. All that they had seen and experienced of God's wondrous works did not enable them to shake off the pagan influence of idols.

Inexplicably, Aaron acquiesced to their request and created a golden calf made out of the gold jewelry the Israelites had carried with them out of Egypt. Not only did they worship this idol, but the Scriptures say they sacrificed burnt offerings and indulged in revelry. God, who saw all of this, told Moses to return to the camp. He said, "Go down, because your people, whom you brought up out of Egypt, have become corrupt. They have been quick to turn away from what I commanded them and have made themselves an idol cast in the shape of a calf. They have bowed down to it and sacrificed to it and have said, 'These are your gods, Israel, who brought you up out of Egypt'" (Exodus 32:7–8, NIV).

(I have described this scene in detail because it is a warning for all of us who want to follow God. None of us are above being tempted and beyond the reach of Satan whose agenda is to interfere with the true worship of God.)

Moses returned to the camp and, in anger, broke the two tablets of stone upon which the Ten Commandments were written. He ground up the golden calf into powder, mixed it with water, and forced the people to drink it. The creation of the golden calf was a great offense in the sight of God, and His wrath was kindled against His people. The first commandment is "I am the Lord your God, who brought you out of the land of Egypt, out of the house of slavery. You shall have no other Gods before Me" (Exodus 20:2–3, NIV). At the very moment it was being written by the hand of God on top of Mt. Sinai, it was being broken down below in the camp. After Moses rebuked the people and his brother, Aaron, once again, He climbed the mountain to talk to God, hoping to appease His anger.

Moses offered himself as a sacrifice to save the Israelites from God's judgment. In this act, Moses revealed the chief characteristic of a great leader—love for the people he is leading and shepherding. God rejected his offer and proposed to make a new nation from Moses which Moses, in turn, rejected.

In order for Moses to be an acceptable sacrifice to God, Moses had to be sinless. Since Moses was born a sinner, just like you and I, he didn't qualify. But someone did qualify and that was Jesus Christ because He was born of a virgin just as it was prophesized in Isaiah 7:14.

After Moses talked to God, God relented and directed Moses and his people to leave Mt. Sinai and travel to Canaan and the Promised Land. Because of the repeated disobedience of the Israelites, it wasn't a direct and short route. What should have been an eleven-day journey took forty years!

Moses set out with approximately two million people to cross a desert. It was a daunting task, to say the least.

They had to face many obstacles—the dry barrenness of the desert, the extreme heat of the day and cold at night, and the necessity of food and water was a constant pressing need.

In spite of God's guidance by the cloud during the day and the pillar of fire at night and His continuing protection and provision, their march was marked by murmuring and complaining against Moses and God; the waters of Marah were bitter (Exodus 15:22–27); the miraculous provision of manna was boring, so boring that God was provoked and rained down quail on them (Exodus 16:11–13); they complained about being thirsty (Exodus 17:1–4); they murmured about how difficult it looked to enter the Promised Land even though God had told them to go in and possess it; and the people complained and wanted to kill Moses and select another leader (Numbers 14:10).

Reading Psalm 78 and 106 gives us a very clear picture of what happened during their wilderness march. In spite of all that God did for them, they were not faithful to Him. Instead of being thankful, they were proud, stubborn, and rebellious. Their disobedience led them to disobey God's instructions. On many occasions, "They did not destroy the peoples as the Lord had commanded them, but they mixed with the nations and learned to do as they did. They served their idols which became a snare to them" (Psalm 106:34–36, NIV).

Their continued disobedience brought God's judgment upon them in the form of many defeats and captivities by their enemies. (For example, the Assyrian captivity from 722–606 BC and the Babylonian captivity from 606–536 BC.)

One of the most striking passages of Scripture which is a glimpse into the heart of God is Jeremiah 2:5. God is speaking through His prophet, Jeremiah, to the Israelites, "How have I failed you, that you strayed so far from Me?"[132]

When I read this passage, it resonated with me because that is exactly what my parents said to me when I became a follower of Jesus. They were deeply wounded, and it was then I understood for the first time that God's heart could be wounded. In the Newer Testament, it is written that God's Holy Spirit can be grieved. That Scripture verse was

132. Jeremiah 2:5, paraphrased by author.

a paradigm shift for me in my understanding of God.

I think it will be helpful to briefly examine the reasons for the Jews' failure to fully embrace all that God had given them.

First, I think they misunderstood the purpose of the Law. It was given to them in order for them to see that they could never keep the Law perfectly. It was intended to show them their need of a Savior. Instead, they sought to earn their right standing with God by their own efforts.

There is a wonderful illustration for us in the Passover story. When God was in the process of delivering the Jews from the slavery of Egypt, He instructed them—during the final plague—to put the blood of an innocent and spotless lamb on the doorposts of their makeshift homes. He told them that when the angel of death came to their homes, God would see the blood, and death would pass over them. Please notice what God did not say. He didn't say, "Put a list of your good works on the doorposts for My review, and if you have enough good works, you will be safe." No, it was the blood of the lamb in the Older Testament, and it is the blood of the lamb in the Newer Testament which God requires. The Passover lamb pointed to the Lamb of God (the Messiah Jesus).

We can't earn our salvation, and we will never be worthy or deserving of it. It is all of His grace and mercy that the Israelites were protected that night. In the same way, those of us who believe in the Messiah Jesus and accept His blood sacrifice for our atonement, we, too, will be protected from death. For us, it is eternal protection.

Because of this fundamental misunderstanding, the Israelites did not receive God's gifts with a spirit of humility. Instead, they became proud and arrogant about being God's chosen people and looked down on others. Pride is the sin God hates the most because it was pride which corrupted Satan's heart and brought about the fall of man. God often says in the Scriptures that He opposes the proud but gives grace to the humble.[133] Pride can be very subtle. It can creep into our hearts and manifest itself in the way we think about ourselves and the way we treat others. How can we think of ourselves as being superior to another

133. James 4:6.

when all that we have has been given to us?

In my opinion, one of the main reasons that the Israelites did not recognize their own Messiah was because their relationship with God was essentially a broken one. Historically, it was marked by their disobedience, rebellion, and unbelief. Jesus, Himself—speaking to the Jews of His day—said, "If you believed Moses, you would believe Me, for he wrote about Me. But since you do not believe what he wrote, how are you going to believe what I say" (John 5:46–47, NIV)?

After the rejection of Jesus by the Jews, did God wring His hands and say, "What am I going to do now?" No. He—being God and not someone to be thwarted—reached out once again. This time, He opened His heart and extended His hand to the Gentile nations. The Gentile Christians were now chosen to be God's instruments. They picked up the banner and are fulfilling God's original call to the Jews. He has commissioned the Christians to be His ambassadors to the whole world, proclaiming who He is.

They are doing what He wanted the Jews to do. It is

the same message and mission under similar circumstances: "go out into a sinful, pagan culture and tell them to repent and be reconciled to Me, their creator. Tell them I love them and that I, Myself, have provided a way to return to Me by sending them a Savior (the Messiah Jesus)."

As Isaiah wrote, "I revealed Myself to those who did not ask for Me; I was found by those who did not seek Me. To a nation that did not call on My name, I said, 'Here am I, here am I.' All day long I have held out My hands to an obstinate people, who walk in ways not good, pursuing their own imaginations, a people who continually provoke Me to My very face" (Isaiah 65:1–3, NIV). The Scripture verses quoted above were written by the Jewish prophet, Isaiah, more than seven hundred years before the birth of Christ.

There is an impressive word picture in the Old Testament of God's provision and plan of redemption in Genesis 22. God tested Abraham's faith and asked him to sacrifice his only son, Isaac, whom he loved. Abraham, by faith, took Isaac to the region of Moriah and prepared to obey God's instructions. On the way, Isaac asked his father, "Where is the lamb for the burnt offering" (Genesis 22:7b, NIV).

Abraham replied, "God Himself will provide the lamb for the burnt offering, my son" (Genesis 22:8, NIV). At the moment he was about to slay Isaac, the angel of the Lord interrupted him, stayed his hand, and said, "Do not lay a hand on the boy... Do not do anything to him. Now, I know that you fear God, because you have not withheld from me your son, your only son" (Genesis 22:12, NIV). Abraham looked around and saw a ram caught in a thicket. He went over, took the ram, and sacrificed it on the altar instead of Isaac. Abraham called the place "The Lord will provide." This was a severe test of someone's faith, but Abraham had a high calling in God's redemptive plan.

So at the appointed time in the history of mankind, prophesied long before it happened, a sovereign, majestic, almighty, and loving God picked up a heavenly bow and arrow and, with His strong right hand, pulled the bow string back as far as it could go. Then, He let go, shooting a gleaming golden arrow into the tiny town of Bethlehem. The arrow's tip is dipped in the precious blood of His Son and has the power to open the portals of paradise to all who believe it was sent from the heart of God.

What do the Scriptures reveal about Israel's future?

As the time of His crucifixion drew near, Jesus sat on a hill overlooking Jerusalem and spoke these words, "Oh, Jerusalem, Jerusalem, you who kill the prophets and stone those sent to you, how often I have longed to gather your children together, as a hen gathers her chicks under her wings, but you were not willing. Look your house is left to you desolate. For I tell you, you will not see Me again until you say, 'Blessed is he who comes in the name of the Lord'" (Mathew 23:37, NIV).

There is a time coming when the nation of Israel will return to God, recognize their mistake, repent, and be fully restored to a forgiving God. This was clearly seen by the Jewish prophet, Zechariah, who was carried forward in time by the spirit of the Lord. "On that day, I will set out to destroy all the nations that attack Jerusalem. And I will pour out on the house of David and the inhabitants of Jerusalem a spirit of grace and supplication. They will look on Me, the one they have pierced, and they will mourn for Him as one mourns for an only child and grieve bitterly for Him as one grieves for a firstborn son. On that day, the weeping in Jerusalem will be great " (Zechariah 12:9–11, NIV).

God, whose intrinsic nature is love, has never given up on His chosen people—the Jews. They still have a special place in His heart. He made promises to Israel's patriarchs (Abraham, Isaac, and Jacob) that included their descendants. He will keep those promises because God is the great promise keeper! The very fact of the existence of Israel today is proof that God has preserved them and has a future plan for them. No other group of people have endured so much for so long and have survived. The reason? God!

One of the promises God made to the Jewish people is their return to the land of Israel. This was fulfilled in 1948. The Jewish prophet, Ezekiel, saw the

Jews scattered and then returning to Israel.[134] Israel does not yet possess all of the land God promised them in His Covenant with Abraham.[135]

God confirmed the promise He made to Abraham with his son Isaac (Genesis 26:3) and to Isaac's son, Jacob (Genesis 28:13). Now, they possess only a portion of it. Someday, they will inherit all of it! God's promises cannot be broken.

As believers in God and followers of Jesus, in a similar way, we are walking the land of His promises. Now, we only possess a portion of His promises. Someday, we will inherit all of them, not because we earned it, not because we are worthy or deserve to, but because God loves us, and all of His promises are sealed with His own precious blood. "It is written: no eye has seen, no ear has heard, no mind has conceived what God has prepared for those who love Him" (1 Corinthians 2:9, NIV).

Someday, there will not be any distinction between Jew and Gentile. There will be only one people of God. The

---

134. Ezekiel 37.
135. Genesis 15:18–21; Joshua 1:4.

wall of separation will be broken, and He will meet with us "above the mercy seat" as He once met with Moses in the tabernacle in the wilderness. All of us can only move onto the ground of salvation through the mercy of God. He saves us from the penalty of sin by His mercy; He clothes us in His righteousness by His mercy; and we are reconciled to Him by His mercy. It is all of His mercy.

The Apostle Paul knew about the mercy of God. He, a high-ranking Jewish leader named Saul, was intercepted by the risen Lord Jesus on the road to Damascus where he was going to capture and kill the Jewish Christians. Later, toward the end of his life, he wrote from a dark and cold prison cell, "For from Him and through Him and to Him are all things. To Him be the glory forever! Amen" (Romans 11:36, NIV).

There is a golden nugget of Scripture in Isaiah 34:1, 6, NIV. It is written, "Look in the scroll of the Lord and read: none of these will be missing, not one will lack her mate." This means that not one of God's prophecies and promises will lack its fulfillment. God's Holy Scriptures confirm their own truthfulness.

Israel's restoration will be a time of great jubilation in heaven and rejoicing on Earth. There will be shouts of exclamation. "The Jews have returned to the God of their fathers!"

Shakespeare wrote, "All the world's a stage and all the men and women merely players. They have their exits and their entrances."[136] The first act of God's story opened with the creation of the world and mankind. There have been many entrances and exits and a lot of drama! But the curtain has not come down as yet. The third and final act will be extraordinary (both good and bad). One of the most exciting scenes will depict Israel surrounded and besieged by her many enemies. The situation looks utterly hopeless, but then, Jesus appears, and He fights for her, delivering her from her Gentile oppressors.

Once again, He makes a way where there is no way, just like He did when He parted the Red Sea for them so many years before. He proves to them and the whole

136. William Shakespeare. *As You Like It*, act II, scene VII (All the World's a Stage), lines 139–141.

world that His love for the Jewish people is enduring and everlasting. Making a way where there is no way is how God signs His name. It is His signature!

Who can understand the ways of God? "For My thoughts are not your thoughts, neither are your ways My ways, declares the Lord. As the heavens are higher than the Earth, so are My ways higher than your ways and My thoughts than your thoughts" (Isaiah 55:8–9, NIV).

The Psalmist, David, wrote, "When I consider Your heavens, the work of Your fingers, the moon and the stars, which You have set in place, what is man that You are mindful of him" (Psalm 8:3, NIV).

I realize that there are scholars and writers more qualified than I, but while they may write as scholars, I write as a witness and testify to what I have seen. Who opened my eyes? The Rabbi from Nazareth who was crucified, buried, and rose again, just as He said He would.

The tears that my parents and I shed is the catalyst for writing this book. I want our very painful experience to have some meaning and purpose. If, by reading these pages, some people come to believe that Jesus is indeed the long-promised Messiah of Israel and accept Him as their Savior, then, our tears will count for eternity.

In the inspired lyrics sung by Steve Green:

God and God alone

Reveals the truth of all we call unknown.

And the best and worst of man

Won't change the Master's Plan.

It's God's and God's alone.[137]

Each of us has a story, and when our life intersects the life of the risen Lord Jesus, He finishes our story in a most wondrous way. Mine will end when I stand on heaven's shores and see my wonderful Savior face-to-face! How will your story end?

---

137. McHugh, Phil and Green, Steve. "God and God Alone [For God and God Alone]". 1986.

We are living in very uncertain and dangerous times. The only certainty that we can cling to is God and His Word as expressed in the Bible. There is nothing to fear because we know the end of the story. It is all written out for us. "In the beginning, God created the heavens and the Earth."[138] These are the very first words in Genesis. The last words in Revelation are, "The grace of the Lord Jesus be with God's people. Amen."[139] In between the first book and the last book of the Bible, the Master Storyteller reveals who He is and gives us a magnificent blueprint whereby we

---

138. Genesis 1:1, NIV.
139. Revelation 22:21, NIV.

may become "His people" in whom He delights. This is the "good news of great joy" that the angel told the shepherds in the field that wondrous night so long ago.[140]

The rapture of the church

I believe the next event on God's calendar is the rapture of the church. This means that all true believers in Jesus Christ will be taken up in the air to be with Jesus. The Word of God says we will be removed from the Earth in a twinkling of an eye. "Listen, I tell you a mystery: we will not all sleep, but we will all be changed—in a flash, in a twinkling of an eye, at the last trumpet. For the trumpet will sound, the dead will be raised imperishable, and we will be changed... Death has been swallowed up in victory" (1 Corinthians 15:51–52, 54b, NIV).

In order to believe this, you must first believe that God exists and that He created the whole universe and its natural laws. Because He created the natural laws, He can suspend them. He has often done this. The whole Bible is the telling of one supernatural event after another.

140. Luke 2:10, ESV.

Let's look at just one example in the Older Testament—Joshua 10:13–14. When Israel was fighting one of their enemies—the Amorites—Joshua spoke to God and asked Him to make the sun and moon stand still. God responded to Joshua's plea, and the sun stood still for about a day, allowing Israel to have the victory.

Our God is sovereign. He created the sun. It moves and stops at His command.

The tribulation period or the time of Jacob's trouble

The Bible prophesies a seven-year period of severe trouble which will afflict the world. Its purpose is to rid the world of evil and to draw men to God. There will be wars, famine, fires, earthquakes, locusts, and one third of the sun, moon, and stars will be darkened. These judgments are very similar to God's judgments on Egypt when He afflicted them with ten plagues.

During the beginning of this period, the Apostle John was given a vision by God (Revelation 7). 144,000 Jews will become believers in Jesus, and God will send them out as

His representatives. They will go out into the whole world proclaiming the truth of the Gospel message of repentance and faith in Jesus Christ. They will be doing what God called the Jewish people to do in the first place when He chose them and set them apart.

They will fulfill their original calling which was to be His special messengers in a pagan world. They will reveal Him to be the only true and living God, offering a sin-darkened world the only hope there is—a restored relationship with Him through His Son, the Messiah.

During the seven-year period of the tribulation, the Antichrist (the counterfeit one) will be very active. While God is drawing people to Himself, the Antichrist will be deceiving people and drawing people away from God. He will be under the control of Satan like Hitler was. It's the age-old conflict. From the very beginning, a battle has been raging between God and Satan, light and darkness, good and evil, truth and lies. In the balance hangs the prize—the souls of men and women. Satan has always wanted to be like God. God kicked him and his angelic followers out of heaven, but his personal agenda has never changed. He still wants to be like God, and he will use lies and deception to fulfill his purpose. He is the grand manipulator and the great deceiver. The only hope for mankind in resisting his wiles is to read God's Word and rest in His faithfulness. The battle is the Lord's.

During this period, the Bible reveals the Antichrist will force everyone to receive a mark on their right hand or forehead in order to buy and sell goods. God's followers, however, remain true to Him and do not take the mark of the beast whose number is 666 (the meaning is not known as yet). Every true believer and follower of Jesus is sealed with God's Holy Spirit. It is a seal which cannot be broken. Since Satan knows he can't break it, he does the next best thing; he tries to counterfeit it.

The Antichrist enters into a seven-year treaty with Israel, but after three and a half years, he breaks it and sets up an image of himself in the temple on Mt. Moriah in Jerusalem. Everyone will see his true character, but it will be too late. He will demand that he be worshipped. All who refuse will be sentenced to death.

It's interesting to note that you can see Satan's desire to be like God is still in play. It has always been his supreme goal. This act is described by the Jewish prophet, Daniel, as an abomination in God's sight.[141]

I can almost hear God saying, "If only My people had turned to Me for help in their hour of crisis instead of signing that seven-year treaty. Why did they sign that treaty and ask a man to help them? Why didn't they turn to Me? Did I ever fail them? [His familiar plaintive cry.] If only they had drawn close to Me, read My Word, and believed in the One I sent, Jesus the Messiah, then their 'peace would have been like a river'" (Isaiah 48:18, NIV).

The Antichrist

God told the Jewish prophet, Daniel, that during the end times, a world dictator would arise. He would be aided by a false prophet who is the head of a religious system. The Antichrist will be a counterfeit. Remember, Satan is a liar and a deceiver.

---

141. Daniel 9:27.

Sometime soon, the Jewish people will take possession of the Temple Mount and build the Third Temple. Daily worship services and the offering of animal sacrifices will be reinstituted as it existed under the Mosaic Law. Preparations are already underway for the building of the temple. Architectural drawings are on the table. When I visited Israel a few years ago, I saw the huge Golden Menorah which will, one day, occupy the temple.

During this period anti-Semitism will increase rapidly, and the Jews' enemies will multiply. Feeling surrounded and overwhelmed, they will reach out to this world dictator, seeking his protection. They will sign a seven-year contract with him which offers them military protection. The signing of this contract marks the beginning of the tribulation period or the time of Jacob's trouble.

What shall we watch for? The Jews retaking the Temple Mount; the building of the Third Temple; the rapid rise of anti-Semitism; and the signing of the seven-year contract.

Some people speculate that the Antichrist will be a very charismatic, powerful, political leader in Europe. He could be alive right now, perhaps in school, not knowing the part he, someday, will play on the world stage.

How will we be able to identify the Antichrist? He will be the one who signs the seven-year contract with Israel.

I believe these events will happen exactly like God said they would (Daniel 9:27; 2 Thessalonians 2:7–8; and Revelation 13:1, NIV). He told us all of this in advance because He loves us and wants us to be prepared.

The battle of Gog and Magog

Sometime, when Israel is at peace, possibly during the first three and a half years of the tribulation period, a huge army from "far north" of Israel will join forces with some other countries and attack Israel. Russia is the furthest country north of Israel. Some of the other countries who join forces with this northern country may be Iran, Turkey, Sudan, and Libya. The Jewish prophet, Ezekiel, describes this war and prophesied that God will supernaturally intervene and fight for Israel.[142] Gog and Magog will be defeated by God, Himself, and it will take seven months to

142. Ezekiel 38–39.

bury all of their dead.[143]

The Jewish people recognize and accept Messiah Jesus and the battle of Armageddon

At the end of the tribulation period, Israel suffers great persecution and is surrounded by her enemies. She is isolated and alone. Many Jews will flee to Edom in the vicinity of Bozrah, Teman, and Petra. Bozrah will be the place of the Jews' last stand.[144]

The Jews will recognize that they are cornered. During this dark hour, they will remember the message of the 144,000 Jewish messengers and turn back to God. He will open the eyes of their understanding, and they will see that they rejected their own Messiah who is Jesus. There shall be mourning in Israel. The Jewish prophet, Zechariah, writes, "And I will pour out on the house of David and the inhabitants of Jerusalem the Spirit of grace [or unmerited favor] and supplications. And they will look on Me, the one they have pierced, and they will mourn for Him, as

---

143. Ezekiel 39:11–12.
144. Micah 2:12.

one mourns for an only child, and grieve bitterly for Him as one grieves for a firstborn son" (Zechariah 12:10, NIV).

They will return to God and pray for His mercy and grace. God responds to their pleas. They will be reborn, and He will put His spirit in them. "And I will put My Spirit within you, and you shall live" (Ezekiel 37:14, ESV). God is a faithful covenant-keeping God. He made promises to the Jewish people when He chose them, and even though they turned their back on Him, He didn't write them off. He wept for them. And He is still weeping for them.

The Scriptures reveal God's broken heart, "O Jerusalem, Jerusalem, you who kill the prophets and stone those sent to you, how often I have longed to gather your children together, as a hen gathers her chicks under her wings, but you were not willing. Look, your house is left to you desolate. For I tell you, you will not seem Me again until you say, 'Blessed is He who comes in the name of the Lord'" (Matthew 23:37–39, NIV). Only someone you deeply love can break your heart.

Shortly after the Jews return to God, Messiah

Jesus returns to Earth to fight for Israel and make war against the Antichrist and his coalition of armies (the battle of Armageddon).

"He will first come to the Jews defense in Bozrah, and they will hail Him, 'Blessed is He who comes in the name of the Lord'" (Matthew 23:39, NIV). Messiah will march triumphantly over His enemies on His way toward His beloved city Jerusalem. The Jewish prophet Zechariah saw the Messiah Jesus standing in victory on the Mount of Olives. "On that day, His feet will stand on the Mount of Olives, east of Jerusalem" (Zechariah 14:4, NIV).

Messiah's great victory will result in Israel becoming the head nation of the world. Then, the world will begin to enjoy the fullness of God's promise to Abraham: "Through your offspring, all nations on Earth will be blessed" (Genesis 22:18, NIV).

In that day, the "Mighty God, Everlasting Father, Prince of Peace"[145] will have established His throne in Jerusalem and "of the greatness of His government and peace there will be no end. He will reign on David's throne

---

145. Isaiah 9:6.

and over His kingdom, establishing and upholding it with justice and righteousness from that time on and forever" (Isaiah 9:7, NIV).

Then, the dark night of the tribulation period or the time of Jacob's trouble will have ended, and the glorious morning of the Golden era will have dawned.[146]

God judges the nations

Messiah Jesus will gather all the nations before Him, and He will separate them from one another "as a shepherd separates the sheep from the goats" (Matthew 25:32, NIV). Those that are in right standing with God (truly born again) will enter into eternal life with God, and those who are not in right standing with God will be sent away into eternal punishment.[147] Hell is real and is a place of eternal torment.

146. Haynie, Burl. *Time of Jacob's Trouble Approaching Israel—God's Timepiece.* (I am indebted to Burl Haynie who was my first Sunday school teacher. He was a kind and gentle man who had a deep understanding of God's Holy Scriptures. He loved the Jewish people and always reminded the class that God called the Jews the apple of His eye. "For he who touches you, touches the apple of His eye" [Zechariah 2:8].)

147. Matthew 25:31–46h.

Satan is thrown into a bottomless pit

God's enemies are defeated and removed from the earthly realm. The Antichrist, the false prophet, and their deceived followers are gone. God's arch enemy, Satan, is thrown into a bottomless pit for one thousand years. Once again, God demonstrates He is sovereign.

The millennial kingdom

Jesus triumphs over His and Israel's enemies. God's anointed Jewish prophets, Isaiah and Micah, prophesied that the Messiah would establish His throne in Jerusalem for one thousand years. Jesus is on the throne in heaven now. During the millennial kingdom, He will be seated on the throne in His beloved city, Jerusalem.

"In the last days, the mountain of the Lord's temple will be established as the highest of the mountains; it will be exalted above the hills, and peoples will stream to it. Many nations will come and say, 'Come, let us go up to the mountain of the Lord, to the temple of the God of Jacob.

He will teach us His ways, so that we may walk in His paths'" (Micah 4:1–2, NIV).

Messiah Jesus will rule with His resurrected believers who have returned with Him. A glorious reign of peace and prosperity will be established on Earth. I think this portion of Scripture gives us a glimpse into the heart of God. I believe it has always been God's heart's desire to fellowship with those He created in His image.

When mankind failed Him in the garden (Adam and Eve represented all of us there), God designed a sacrificial system, so a Holy God and a sinful people would not be separated forever. This design was seen in the tabernacle in the wilderness, the temple, and finally, on the cross. It opened a way back—a bridge—to restored fellowship with God. Even though mankind has repeatedly and rebelliously turned their back on God, God has never given up on us.

Jesus said, "Anyone who has seen Me has seen the Father" (John 14:9, NIV). Scripture offers us a wonderful image. It reveals that the Son (Jesus) is the *out raying* or radiance of the divine.[148] The rays of God's heavenly power

148. Hebrews 1:3.

and unconditional love, emanating from the heart of God, took shape and found expression in an earthly body. Jesus was sent by the Father to reveal who God is and tell the whole world that God loves us.

When God said to Joshua, "I will never leave you or forsake you,"[149] I believe He was revealing the deepest part of His heart—the very essence of His being, which is love. Divine love. Unconditional and everlasting love. That promise made so long ago is true today. Every born-again believer in the Messiah Jesus receives God's Holy Spirit and becomes the temple in which He resides.

Satan's last hurrah

Satan is released from the pit at the end of the one thousand years. One may wonder why this occurs, but God says in the Scriptures that "My thoughts are not your thoughts, neither are your ways My ways" (Isaiah 55:8, NIV). In a final attempt to overthrow God, Satan will assemble a coalition of nations from the four corners of the Earth. They will surround "the camp of God's people,

149. Joshua 1:5, NIV.

the city He loves."[150] This is Jerusalem. Once again, God demonstrates His unshakeable love and commitment to His people. He sends down fire from heaven and consumes His enemies. The devil is thrown into the lake of fire and sulfur where the Antichrist and the false prophet are "where they will be tormented day and night forever and ever" (Revelation 20:10, NIV). The battle is over, and Jesus is Lord!

The great white throne judgment

At the time of the writing of the final book of the Bible—Revelation—John, the beloved disciple of Jesus, was in exile on the island of Patmos. God used this time of solitude to reveal Himself and the end times to him. In the last pages of the book, John wrote that he saw a great white throne and One who was seated on it. He saw "the dead, great and small, standing before the throne, and books were opened. Another book was opened, which is the book of life. The dead were judged according to what they had done as recorded... anyone whose name was not

---

150. Revelation 20:9.

found written in the book of life was thrown into the lake of fire" (Revelation 20:12, 15, NIV).

For the believer, it will be a throne of grace; but for the unbeliever, it will be a throne of judgment. There will be two separate judgments—one for believers and one for unbelievers. Everyone will stand and give an account of his life to a holy and righteous Judge. It won't matter whether you are rich or poor, male or female, old or young, educated or illiterate. The only thing that will matter is whether or not you accepted or rejected Jesus. That's God's standard.

I am reminded of the story of the Titanic. On that ill-fated ship, there were many different groups of people. There were the rich and the poor (divided into three classes), the educated and uneducated, the famous and unknown, and those with diverse ethnic backgrounds. After the ship sank, the only thing that mattered was the passenger list which was posted. There were only two categories on that list: those who were lost and those who were saved. And that's all that will matter at the judgment seat of God. So on our life's journey, as we ponder "things that matter," let us consider what matters to God. That will be the only thing that matters!

The new heaven and the new Earth

In order to understand the end of the Bible, we need to return to the beginning. The words we read in the first book of the Torah, Genesis, are: "In the beginning God created the heavens and the Earth" (Genesis 1:1, NIV). In the last book of the Bible—Revelation—God reveals to His servant, John, that He will recreate the heavens and the Earth.[151] In between are many stories of God's redeeming love. He is the Storyteller, and He uses real people and events, punctuated by His supernatural interventions.

The whole Bible which contains the Older and Newer Testaments is one book, written by one Author—God. He used men as His instruments to write the sixty-six books of the Bible, but they were guided and superintended by His Holy Spirit.[152]

The Bible has been laughed at, mocked, ridiculed, and

---

151. Revelation 21:1.
152. 2 Peter 1:20–21.

scorned, yet it still endures. Like a huge solid rock which cannot be moved, it will never be shaken because God's strong right hand holds it firmly in place.[153] The Bible's story originated in the heart of a loving God and was shot like an arrow from heaven to Earth. Throughout the centuries, people have been drawn to it like a magnet. Why? I think it is because some of us recognize our Creator's voice. Sadly, many do not.

When Jesus asked Peter, "Who do you say that I am" (Matthew 16:15, NIV).

Peter replied, "You are the Messiah, the Son of the living God" (Matthew 16:16, NIV).

It was God who had opened Peter's eyes and enabled him to recognize who Jesus was. God will do the same for each one of us because He says, "You will seek Me and find Me, when you search for Me with all your heart" (Jeremiah 29:13, NKJV).

John, exiled on the Island of Patmos, says he was "in the spirit" and carried forward in time to see future events. At the close of the book, he said, "Then, I saw a new heaven

153. Isaiah 40:8.

and new Earth, for the first heaven and the first Earth had passed away [vanished], and the sea was no more. And I saw the holy city, the New Jerusalem, descending out of heaven from God" (Revelation 21:1–2, ESV).

Then, John heard a voice from the throne saying, "Behold, the dwelling place of God is with man. He will dwell with them, and they will be His people, and God Himself will be with them as their God" (Revelation 21:3, ESV). This fulfills what the Jewish prophet, Ezekiel, prophesized, "My dwelling place [or tabernacle] shall be with them, and I will be their God, and they shall be My people" (Ezekiel 37:27, ESV).

When Adam and Eve fell from grace in the garden and all looked lost, God had a plan. God always has a plan. He created everything there is and stands outside of His creation as sovereign ruler. He has no intention of letting Satan have the final victory, and He won't let Satan have the victory in our lives. If we belong to Him by faith in Messiah Jesus, we are His people and part of His victorious redemption and restoration plan.

John continues to explain what will happen on that great day. "He will wipe every tear from their eyes. There will be no more death or mourning or crying or pain" (Revelation 21:4, NIV).

The Jewish prophet, Isaiah, wrote a similar prophecy. "He [the Messiah] will swallow up death forever [in victory, He will abolish death forever]. And the Lord God will wipe away tears from all faces; and the reproach of His people He will take away from off all the Earth; for the Lord has spoken it" (Isaiah 25:8, ESV).

Isaiah lived seven hundred years before the birth of John. Do you hear the voice of the Storyteller speaking to both of them?

There are many golden nuggets in the Bible. Here is another one written by Isaiah: "Seek out of the book of the Lord and read: not one of these [details of prophecy] will be missing, none will lack its mate [in fulfillment]" (Isaiah 34:16, NASB). The Scriptures declares its own truthfulness.

What else did God reveal to John? John described

the New Jerusalem: "It's radiance like a most rare jewel, like a jasper, clear as crystal. It had a great high wall with twelve gates, and at the gates, twelve angels, and on the gates the names of the twelve tribes of the sons of Israel were inscribed... And the wall of the city had twelve foundations [stones], and on them the twelve names of the twelve apostles of the Lamb... And the twelve gates were twelve pearls, each of the gates made of a single pearl. And the street of the city was pure gold like transparent glass" (Revelation 21:11–12, 14, 21, ESV).

John continues, "And I saw no temple in the city, for its temple is the Lord God the Almighty and the Lamb. And the city had no need of sun or moon to shine on it, for the glory of God gives it light, and its lamp is the Lamb" (Revelation 21:22–23, ESV).

Earlier, the Jewish prophet, Isaiah, wrote, "The sun shall be no more your light by day, nor for brightness shall the moon give you light, but the Lord will be your everlasting light... And your days of your mourning shall be ended" (Isaiah 60:19–20, ESV).

Once again, God's Holy Spirit carried both the Jewish prophet, Isaiah, and the Newer Testament apostle, John, forward in time and gave both of them a similar vision of the future! One Holy Spirit, one Voice, one Storyteller, *one book*!

As John concludes the final book of Revelation and the Bible's story, the Storyteller (God) enables John to see "the river of the water of life, bright as crystal, flowing from the throne of God and of the Lamb... On either side of the river, the tree of life with its twelve kinds of fruit... The leaves of the tree were for the healing of the nations" (Revelation 22:1–2, ESV).

The curse originally placed on Earth after the fall is removed, and God's people see Him face-to-face and worship Him with joyful adoration forever and ever. Who will be able to enter the New Jerusalem? "*Only those whose names are written in the lamb's book of life*" (Revelation 21:27, NIV).

This may disturb some people, but God is not concerned with being politically correct. He is holy, righteous, and just, and the New Jerusalem is His city. He decides who will live with Him there forever and ever. He did make a way for you and me to enter that city. It is by His invitation. *Only* by the shed blood of His beloved Son and Messiah, Jesus, can someone enter the golden city. The invitation is sent to everyone.

At the top of the invitation, God engraved these words: "For God so loved the world, that he gave his only Son that whoever believes in him should not perish but have eternal life."[154] At the bottom of the invitation is printed RSVP. What will be your reply?

I conclude my little book with a story I once heard:

A man was lying on his bed. He was very near death and drifting in and out of sleep. His beloved daughter was sitting nearby in a chair reading the Bible. The man slowly opened his eyes and beckoned her to come closer to him. He wanted to tell her something. His daughter rose from the chair, walked toward her father's bed, and leaned over so she could hear him. Her father was breathing with difficulty. With great effort, he managed to utter only two words in a whisper. The daughter heard her father say, "*Be*

---

154. John 3:16, ESV.

there!" Then, he closed his eyes and died.

That's my prayer for you, dear reader. The Bible's story of mankind concludes with a glorious finish, and the dawn of a new age will begin. *Be there!*

"The grass withers, the flowers fade, but the Word of our God will stand forever" (Isaiah 40:8, ESV)

"Seek and read from the book of the Lord: not one of these shall be missing: none shall be without her mate" (Isaiah 34:16a, NIV).[155]

---

155 It can be interpreted that this verse means that every prophecy will have its fulfillment.

| As It Is Written (in the Older Testament) | As It Was Fulfilled (in the Newer Testament) |

The Messiah Would Be Born in Bethlehem

But you, Bethlehem Ephrathah, though you are small among the clans of Judah, out of you will come for me one who will be ruler over Israel, whose origins are from of old, from ancient times. (Micah 5:2, NIV

So Joseph also went up from the town of Nazareth in Galilee to Judea, to Bethlehem the town of David, because he belonged to the house and line of David. He went there to register with Mary, who was pledged to be married to him and was expecting a child. While they were there, the time came for the baby to be born, and she gave birth to her firstborn, a Son. She wrapped Him in cloths and placed Him in a manger, because there was no room for them in the inn. (Luke 2:4–7, NIV)

| As It Is Written | As It Was Fulfilled |
| (in the Older Testament) | (in the Newer Testament) |

Born of a Virgin

Therefore, the Lord Himself will give you a sign: the virgin will be with child and will give birth to a Son and will call Him *Immanuel*†. (Isaiah 7:14, NIV)

In the sixth month of Elizabeth's pregnancy, God sent the Angel Gabriel to Nazareth, a town in Galilee, to a virgin pledged to be married to a man named Joseph, a descendant of David. The virgin's name was Mary. The angel went to her and said, "Greetings, you who are highly favored! The Lord is with you... You will be with child and give birth to a Son, and you are to give Him the name Jesus. He will be great and will be called the Son of the Most High. (Luke 1:26–27, 31–32, NIV

| As It Is Written | As It Was Fulfilled |
| (in the Older Testament) | (in the Newer Testament) |

A Descendant of Judah

The scepter will not depart from Judah, nor the ruler's staff from between his feet, until He comes to whom it belongs, and the obedience of the nations is His. (Genesis 49:10, NIV)

Jesus was the direct descendant from the tribe of Judah. (Luke 3:21–33, NIV)

---

† *Immanuel*- literally, God with us.

As It Is Written (in the Older Testament)	As It Was Fulfilled (in the Newer Testament)

The Messiah's First Spiritual Work Will Be in Galilee

Nevertheless, there will be no more gloom for those who were in distress. In the past He humbled the land of Zebulun and the land of Naphtali, but in the future, He will honor Galilee of the nations, by the way of the sea, along the Jordan—the people walking in darkness have seen a great light. (Isaiah 9:1–2a, NIV)

When Jesus heard that John had been put in prison, He returned to Galilee. Leaving Nazareth, He went and lived in Capernaum, which was by the lake in the area of Zebulun and Naphtali, to fulfill what was said through the prophet Isaiah… From that time on Jesus began to preach, repent, for the kingdom of heaven is near. (Matthew 4:12–14, 17, NIV)

As It Is Written (in the Older Testament)	As It Was Fulfilled (in the Newer Testament)

The Messiah Will Make the Blind See, the Deaf Hear, Etc.

Then will the eyes of the blind be opened and the ears of the deaf unstopped. Then will the lame leap like a deer, and the mute tongue shout for joy. Water will gush forth in the wilderness and streams in the desert. (Isaiah 35:5–6 NIV)

Jesus replied, "Go back and report to John what you hear and see: the blind receive sight, the lame walk, those who have leprosy are cured, the deaf hear, the dead are raised, and the good news is preached to the poor." (Matthew 11:4–5, NIV)

| As It Is Written (in the Older Testament) | As It Was Fulfilled (in the Newer Testament) |

The Messiah Will Enter Jerusalem Riding on a Donkey

"Rejoice greatly, O Daughter Zion! Shout, Daughter of Jerusalem! See, your king comes to you, righteous and having salvation, gentle and riding on a donkey, on a colt, the foal of a donkey."

(Zechariah 9:9 NIV)

"The disciples went and did as Jesus had instructed them. They brought the donkey and the colt and placed their cloaks on them for Jesus and he sat on them. A very large crowd spread their cloaks on the road, while others cut branches from the trees and spread them on the road. The crowds that went ahead of him and those that followed shouted, Hosanna to the Son of David! Blessed is he who comes in the name of the Lord! Hosanna in the highest.!" (Matthew 21:6-9 NIV)

| As It Is Written (in the Older Testament) | As It Was Fulfilled (in the Newer Testament) |

The Messiah Will Be Silent in Front of His Accusers

He was oppressed and afflicted, yet He did not open His mouth; He was led like a lamb to the slaughter, and as a sheep before her shearers is silent, so He did not open his mouth. (Isaiah 53:7, NIV)

Then the high priest stood up and said to Jesus, "Are You not going to answer? What is this testimony that these men are bringing against You?" But Jesus remained silent. (Matthew 26:62–63, NIV)

| As It Is Written (in the Older Testament) | As It Was Fulfilled (in the Newer Testament) |

The Messiah Would Be Betrayed By a Friend

My close friend, someone I trusted, one who shared my bread has lifted up his heel against me. (Psalm 1:9

"I am not referring to all of you, I know those I have chosen. But this is to fulfill the Scripture. He who shares My bread has lifted up his heel against Me." After He had said this, Jesus was troubled in spirit and testified, "I tell you the truth, one of you is going to betray Me." (John 13:18, 21, NIV)

| As It Is Written (in the Older Testament) | As It Was Fulfilled (in the Newer Testament) |

The Messiah Will Be Sold for Thirty Pieces of Silver

"I told them, 'If you think it best, give me my pay; but if not, keep it.' So they paid me thirty pieces of silver. And the LORD said to me, 'Throw it to the potter—the handsome price at which they priced Me!' So I took the thirty pieces of silver and threw them into the house of the Lord to the potter." (Zechariah 11:12–13, NIV

Then, one of the twelve—the one called Judas Iscariot—went to the chief priests and asked, "What are you willing to give me if I hand Him over to you?" So they counted out for him thirty silver coins. From then on, Judas watched for an opportunity to hand Him over. (Matthew 26:14–16, NIV)

As It Is Written (in the Older Testament)	As It Was Fulfilled (in the Newer Testament)

The Messiah Will Be Beaten, Mocked, and Spat Upon

"I offered My back to those who beat Me, My cheeks to those who pulled out My beard; I did not hide My face from mocking and spitting." (Isaiah 50:6, NIV	They stripped Him and put a scarlet robe on Him, then twisted together a crown of thorns and set it on His head. They put a staff in His right hand and knelt in front of Him and mocked Him. "Hail, King of the Jews!" they said. They spit on Him and took the staff and struck Him on the head again and again. (Matthew 27:28–31, NIV

As It Is Written (in the Older Testament)	As It Was Fulfilled (in the Newer Testament)

The Messiah Will Be Accused by False Witnesses

"Ruthless witnesses come forward; they question me on things I know nothing about. They repay me evil for good and leave my soul forlorn." (Psalm 35:11–12, NIV)	The chief priests and the whole Sanhedrin were looking for evidence against Jesus so that they could put Him to death, but they did not find any. Many testified falsely against Him, but their statements did not agree. (Mark 14:55–56, NIV)

As It Is Written (in the Older Testament)	As It Was Fulfilled (in the Newer Testament)

The Messiah Would Be Crucified

Note: Crucifixion was not the usual way people were executed. It was invented by the Romans hundreds of years after this prophecy was written.

"A band of evil men has encircled Me; they have pierced My hands and My feet." (Psalm 22:16, NIV)	When they came to the place which is called the Skull, there they crucified Him. (Luke 23:33)

As It Is Written (in the Older Testament)	As It Was Fulfilled (in the Newer Testament)

He Was Given Vinegar and Gall to Drink

"They put gall in My food and gave Me vinegar for My thirst." (Psalm 69:21, NIV)	They gave Him vinegar to drink, mingled with gall. (Matthew 27:34, NASB)

As It Is Written (in the Older Testament)	As It Was Fulfilled (in the Newer Testament)

The Soldiers Gambled for His Coat

"They divide My garments among them and cast lots for My clothing." (Psalm 22:18, NIV)	Jesus said, "Father, forgive them, for they do not know what they are doing." And they divided up His clothes by casting lots. (Luke 23:34, NIV)

As It Is Written (in the Older Testament)	As It Was Fulfilled (in the Newer Testament)
He Would Be Crucified with Sinners	
"Therefore, I will give Him a portion among the great, and He will divide the spoils with the strong, because He poured out His life unto death, and was numbered with the transgressors. For He bore the sin of many and made intercession for the transgressors." (Isaiah 53:12, NIV)	And they crucified two robbers with Him, one on His right and one on His left. (Mark 15:27, NIV)

As It Is Written (in the Older Testament)	As It Was Fulfilled (in the Newer Testament)

Not One of the Bones of the Messiah Would Be Broken

Note: A person's legs were usually broken after being crucified to speed up their death.

He keeps all His bones, not one of them is broken, (Psalm 34:20, NASB)	But when they came to Jesus and saw that He was already dead, they did not break His legs. (John 19:33, NIV)

As It Is Written (in the Older Testament)	As It Was Fulfilled (in the Newer Testament)

He Would Be Burried with the Rich

And they made His grave with the wicked and with the rich in His death. (Isaiah 53:9, ESV)

When it was evening, there came a rich man from Arimathea, named Joseph, who also a disciple of Jesus. He went to Pilate and asked for the body of Jesus. Then, Pilate ordered it to be given to him. And Joseph took the body and wrapped it in a clean linen shroud and laid it in his own new tomb which he had cut in the rock. (Matthew 27:57–60a, NIV)

As It Is Written (in the Older Testament)	As It Was Fulfilled (in the Newer Testament)

The Messiah Will Ascend to His Father's Right Hand

The Lord says to my Lord; "Sit at My right hand." (Psalm 110:1, NIV)

"After the Lord Jesus had spoken to them, he was taken up into heaven and he sat at the right hand of God." (Mark 16:19, NIV) ‡

---

‡ Jesus appeared to the disciples after His resurrection, as well as to *many others*

As It Is Written (in the Older Testament)	As It Was Fulfilled (in the Newer Testament)

The Messiah Will Be the Son of God

Therefore, you kings, be wise; be warned, you rulers of the Earth. Serve the LORD with fear and rejoice with trembling. Kiss the Son, lest He be angry, and you be destroyed in your way, for His wrath can flare up in a moment. Blessed are all who take refuge in Him. (Psalm 2:10–12, NIV)	At that time, Jesus came from Nazareth in Galilee and was baptized by John in the Jordan. As Jesus was coming up out of the water, He saw heaven being torn open and the Spirit descending on Him like a dove. And a voice came from heaven: "You are My Son, whom I love; with You I am well pleased." (Mark 1:9–11, NIV)

As It Is Written (in the Older Testament)	As It Was Fulfilled (in the Newer Testament)

The Messiah Will Be Killed

Surely, He took up our infirmities and carried our sorrows, yet we considered Him stricken by God, smitten by Him, and afflicted. But He was pierced for our transgressions, He was crushed for our iniquities; the punishment that brought us peace was upon Him, and by His wounds we are healed. (Isaiah 53:4–5 NIV; This was written by the Jewish prophet, Isaiah approximately seven hundred years before the birth of Jesus!)	With a loud cry, Jesus breathed His last. The curtain of the temple was torn in two from top to bottom. And when the centurion, who stood there in front of Jesus, heard His cry and saw how He died, he said, "Surely, this man was the Son of God." (Mark 15:37–39, NIV)

o The sacrifices mentioned in the Older Testament were only meant to atone temporarily for the sins of the people. They were only a covering. That is why Yom Kippur is observed every year. Please note the words that John the Baptist used when he recognized Jesus as the Messiah: "Look, the Lamb of God who *takes away* the sin of the world" (John 1:29, NIV).

o I think it is also interesting to note that in the Holy Room of the Tabernacle, where the Ark of the Covenant was kept, there wasn't a chair. The high priest could not sit down. His work was never finished. However, when Jesus entered the Holy of Holies (heaven) on our behalf, He is described as "seated" at the right hand of God (Mark 16:19, NIV). That's because His work was, in His own words, "finished" (John 19:30, NIV).

To God Be the Glory

Jesus Christ carried the cross, took the blows, and died so that I and all who believe in Him may be unshackled from the chains of sin. I have been rescued, ransomed, and set free to enjoy eternal life with Him forever. The ransom was paid in full by His precious blood. Who can understand such things, and how can I say thanks?

Each of us has a story to tell and so does God. Someone described it as "the greatest story ever told." And it begins in the first book of the Torah. The scarlet thread of redemption weaves its way through the prophetic pages of the Older Testament, finding its fulfillment in the death of the Messiah Jesus on the cross in the Newer Testament.

On the cover of this book, I chose to illustrate the Star of David with a cross in the center. For some Jewish people, that image may be offensive. I understand that. But for me, it means that the sacrifice of the Messiah was always meant to be the central message of Judaism. The Messianic prophecies in the Jewish scriptures point to the Lamb of God (the Messiah) whose blood would be shed for our sins. That message was supposed to be Judaism's fundamental truth. It was God's original plan that it would be the Jewish people who would offer to the whole world His magnificent gift of restoration and redemption.

The Scriptures reveal that, sometime in the future, they will be given another chance to do so. On that great day, if you could see through the clouds, you would see God with a big smile on His face! Only God can redeem the past.

Jesus told the Samaritan woman He met at the well, "Everyone who drinks this water [from the well] will be thirsty again, but whoever drinks the water I give them will never thirst. Indeed, the water I give them will become in them a spring of water welling up to eternal life" (John 4:13–14, NIV). He also told her He was the Messiah!

I love You, Lord Jesus. "Thine is the kingdom, the power, and the glory, forever and ever" (Mathew 6:13, KJV).

If you wish to contact the author: marilyngail7@gmail.com